P1-A1 Ciminelli's
a–g.

_____

_____

_____

_____

_____

_____

_____

_____

_____

_____

_____

_____

_____

_____

_____

_____

_____

_____

_____

_____

_____

_____

_____

_____

_____

_____

_____

_____

P1-A1 Concluded

P1-A2 Richard Parker

a–b.

	CASH	ACCOUNTS RECEIVABLE	OFFICE FURNITURE	VAN	=	ACCOUNTS PAYABLE	+	(+) INVESTMENTS (–) WITHDRAWALS	(+) REVENUES (–) EXPENSES
		ASSETS				LIABILITIES		OWNER'S EQUITY	
1									
2									
3									
4									
5									
6									
7									
8									
9									
10									
11									

P1-A2   Concluded

c.

P1-A3 Grimball Cardiology

a.

Grimball Cardiology

Income Statement

For the Year Ended December 31, 19X1

P1-A3 Continued

b.

Grimball Cardiology

Statement of Owner's Equity

For the Year Ended December 31, 19X1

P1-A3 Continued

c.

Grimball Cardiology

Balance Sheet

December 31, 19X1

P1-A3 Concluded

P1-A5 Decor and More

a.

Decor and More

Income Statement

For the Month Ended May 31, 19X9

P1-A5 Continued

b.

Decor and More

Statement of Owner's Equity

For the Month Ended May 31, 19X9

P1-A5 Continued

c.

Decor and More

Balance Sheet

May 31, 19X9

P1-A5 Concluded

P1-A6 Action Tree Service

P1-A6   Concluded

P1-B1 Hartford Company

a–g.

_____
_____
_____
_____
_____
_____
_____
_____
_____
_____
_____
_____
_____
_____
_____
_____
_____
_____
_____
_____
_____
_____
_____
_____
_____
_____
_____
_____
_____
_____

P1-B1   Concluded

P1-B2 John McCarthy

a–b.

	ASSETS			=	LIABILITIES	+	OWNER'S EQUITY	
	CASH	ACCOUNTS RECEIVABLE	OFFICE EQUIPMENT	TRUCK	ACCOUNTS PAYABLE		(+) INVESTMENTS (−) WITHDRAWALS	(+) REVENUES (−) EXPENSES
1								
2								
3								
4								
5								
6								
7								
8								
9								
10								
11								

P1-B2 Concluded

c.

P1-B3 Essex and Associates

a.

Essex and Associates

Income Statement

For the Year Ended December 31, 19XX

P1-B3 Continued

b.

Essex and Associates

Statement of Owner's Equity

For the Year Ended December 31, 19XX

P1-B3 Continued

c.

Essex and Associates

Balance Sheet

December 31, 19XX

P1-B3 Concluded

P1-B4 Bates Company

a.

	ASSETS				=	LIABILITIES	+	OWNER'S EQUITY	
	CASH	ACCOUNTS RECEIVABLE	LAND	EQUIPMENT		ACCOUNTS PAYABLE		(+) INVESTMENTS (−) WITHDRAWALS	(+) REVENUES (−) EXPENSES
June 2									
3									
4									
5									
8									
11									
17									
18									
20									
23									
28									
30									

P1-B4 Continued

b.

Bates Company

Income Statement

For the Month Ended June 30, 19X5

P1-B4 Continued

b.

Bates Company

Statement of Owner's Equity

For the Month Ended June 30, 19X5

P1-B4 Concluded

b.

Bates Company

Balance Sheet

June 30, 19X1

P1-B5 Jeffcote Advertising Agency

a.

Jeffcote Advertising Agency

Income Statement

For the Month Ended January 31, 19X3

P1-B5 Continued

b.

Jeffcote Advertising Agency

Statement of Owner's Equity

For the Month Ended January 31, 19X3

Name _____

P1-B5   Continued

c.

Jeffcote Advertising Agency
Balance Sheet
January 31, 19X3

P1-B5   Concluded

P1-B6   Rapid Cleaning Service

P1-B6   Concluded

EYH1-1   Starting a Business

a–d.

EYH1-1   Concluded

EYH1-2 Accounting and Regulation

EYH1-2   Concluded

EYH1-3   A Day in the Life . . .

_____

_____

_____

_____

_____

_____

_____

_____

_____

_____

_____

_____

_____

_____

_____

_____

_____

_____

_____

_____

_____

_____

_____

_____

_____

_____

_____

EYH1-3   Concluded

EYH1-4 Ethics and Behavior

EYH1-4   Concluded

EYH1-5 Promus Companies

a–e.

EYH1-5   Concluded

EYH1-6

a–e.

EYH1-6   Concluded

EYH1-7   The Outdoor Store

a–d.

EYH1-7   Concluded

CAI1-1 Wm. Wrigley Jr. Company

a–d.

CAI1-1 Concluded

P2-A1 Mike Scott

P2-A1 Concluded

P2-A2 Delgado Enterprises

a.

Cash		Accounts Receivable

Office Supplies		Office Furniture

Accounts Payable		Roy Delgado, Capital

Roy Delgado, Drawing		Service Revenue

Wage Expense		Advertising Expense

P2-A2 Concluded

b.

Delgado Enterprises

Trial Balance

March 31, 19XX

P2-A3 Adkins Studio

a.

JOURNAL   PAGE _____

	DATE		DESCRIPTION	POST REF.	DEBIT	CREDIT	
1							1
2							2
3							3
4							4
5							5
6							6
7							7
8							8
9							9
10							10
11							11
12							12
13							13
14							14
15							15
16							16
17							17
18							18
19							19
20							20
21							21
22							22
23							23
24							24
25							25
26							26
27							27
28							28
29							29
30							30
31							31
32							32

P2-A3 Continued

b–c.

CASH   ACCOUNT 110

DATE		EXPLANATION	POST REF.	DEBIT	CREDIT	BALANCE

ACCOUNTS RECEIVABLE   ACCOUNT 120

DATE		EXPLANATION	POST REF.	DEBIT	CREDIT	BALANCE

EQUIPMENT & SUPPLIES   ACCOUNT130

DATE		EXPLANATION	POST REF.	DEBIT	CREDIT	BALANCE

P2-A3 Continued

b–c.

STUDIO _____ ACCOUNT 140

DATE		EXPLANATION	POST REF.	DEBIT	CREDIT	BALANCE

ACCOUNTS PAYABLE _____ ACCOUNT 210

DATE		EXPLANATION	POST REF.	DEBIT	CREDIT	BALANCE

LEE ADKINS, CAPITAL _____ ACCOUNT 310

DATE		EXPLANATION	POST REF.	DEBIT	CREDIT	BALANCE

P2-A3 Continued

b–c.

LEE ADKINS, DRAWING   ACCOUNT 320

DATE	EXPLANATION	POST REF.	DEBIT	CREDIT	BALANCE

PROFESSIONAL FEES   ACCOUNT 410

DATE	EXPLANATION	POST REF.	DEBIT	CREDIT	BALANCE

ADVERTISING EXPENSE   ACCOUNT 510

DATE	EXPLANATION	POST REF.	DEBIT	CREDIT	BALANCE

P2-A3 Continued

b–c.

SALARIES EXPENSE   ACCOUNT 520

DATE	EXPLANATION	POST REF.	DEBIT	CREDIT	BALANCE

LEGAL & ACCOUNTING EXPENSE   ACCOUNT 530

DATE	EXPLANATION	POST REF.	DEBIT	CREDIT	BALANCE

UTILITIES EXPENSE   ACCOUNT 540

DATE	EXPLANATION	POST REF.	DEBIT	CREDIT	BALANCE

P2-A3 Concluded

d.

Adkins Studio

Trial Balance

June 30, 19XX

P2-A4 Molly's Landscape

a.

JOURNAL

	DATE		DESCRIPTION	POST REF.	DEBIT	CREDIT	
1							1
2							2
3							3
4							4
5							5
6							6
7							7
8							8
9							9
10							10
11							11
12							12
13							13
14							14
15							15
16							16
17							17
18							18
19							19
20							20
21							21
22							22
23							23
24							24
25							25
26							26
27							27
28							28
29							29
30							30
31							31
32							32

P2-A4 Continued

b.

CASH   ACCOUNT 110

DATE	EXPLANATION	POST REF.	DEBIT	CREDIT

ACCOUNTS RECEIVABLE   ACCOUNT 120

DATE	EXPLANATION	POST REF.	DEBIT	CREDIT

OFFICE EQUIPMENT   ACCOUNT 130

DATE	EXPLANATION	POST REF.	DEBIT	CREDIT

P2-A4 Continued

b.

ACCOUNTS PAYABLE   ACCOUNT 210

DATE		EXPLANATION	POST REF.	DEBIT	CREDIT	BALANCE

OTHER LIABILITIES   ACCOUNT 220

DATE		EXPLANATION	POST REF.	DEBIT	CREDIT	BALANCE

MOLLY GREGG, CAPITAL   ACCOUNT 310

DATE		EXPLANATION	POST REF.	DEBIT	CREDIT	BALANCE

P2-A4 Continued

b.

LANDSCAPING REVENUE

ACCOUNT 410

DATE	EXPLANATION	POST REF.	DEBIT	CREDIT	BALANCE

RENT EXPENSE

ACCOUNT 510

DATE	EXPLANATION	POST REF.	DEBIT	CREDIT	BALANCE

SECRETARIAL EXPENSE

ACCOUNT 520

DATE	EXPLANATION	POST REF.	DEBIT	CREDIT	BALANCE

P2-A4 Continued

b.

UTILITIES EXPENSE   ACCOUNT 530

DATE		EXPLANATION	POST REF.	DEBIT	CREDIT	BALANCE

                                                                          ACCOUNT

DATE		EXPLANATION	POST REF.	DEBIT	CREDIT	BALANCE

                                                                          ACCOUNT

DATE		EXPLANATION	POST REF.	DEBIT	CREDIT	BALANCE

P2-A4 Concluded

c.

Molly's Landscaping Service

Trial Balance

January 31, 19XX

P2-A5 Muniserv

a.

JOURNAL

	DATE		DESCRIPTION	POST REF.	DEBIT	CREDIT	
1							1
2							2
3							3
4							4
5							5
6							6
7							7
8							8
9							9
10							10
11							11
12							12
13							13
14							14
15							15
16							16
17							17
18							18
19							19
20							20
21							21
22							22
23							23
24							24
25							25
26							26
27							27
28							28
29							29
30							30
31							31
32							32

P2-A5 Concluded

b–c.

P2-B1 Coal Mine Pale Ale

a. and c.

P2-B1 Concluded

b.

P2-B2 Lopez Service

a.

Cash		Accounts Receivable	

Office Equipment		Land	

Accounts Payable		Loan Payable	

Lopez, Capital		Service Revenue	

Advertising Expense		Salaries Expense	

Utilities Expense	

P2-B2 Concluded

b.

Lopez Service Organization

Trial Balance

May 31, 19XX

P2-B4 AAA Furniture Leasing

a.

JOURNAL   PAGE _____

	DATE		DESCRIPTION	POST REF.	DEBIT	CREDIT	
1							1
2							2
3							3
4							4
5							5
6							6
7							7
8							8
9							9
10							10
11							11
12							12
13							13
14							14
15							15
16							16
17							17
18							18
19							19
20							20
21							21
22							22
23							23
24							24
25							25
26							26
27							27
28							28
29							29
30							30
31							31
32							32

P2-B4 Continued

b.

CASH

DATE	EXPLANATION	POST REF.	DEBIT	CREDIT	BALANCE

ACCOUNTS RECEIVABLE ACCOUNT 120

DATE	EXPLANATION	POST REF.	DEBIT	CREDIT	BALANCE

RENTAL FURNITURE ACCOUNT 130

DATE	EXPLANATION	POST REF.	DEBIT	CREDIT	BALANCE

P2-B4 Continued

b.

ACCOUNTS PAYABLE   ACCOUNT 210

DATE		EXPLANATION	POST REF.	DEBIT	CREDIT	BALANCE

LOAN PAYABLE   ACCOUNT 220

DATE		EXPLANATION	POST REF.	DEBIT	CREDIT	BALANCE

JAMES LARKIN, CAPITAL   ACCOUNT 300

DATE		EXPLANATION	POST REF.	DEBIT	CREDIT	BALANCE

P2-B4 Continued

b.

RENTAL REVENUE   ACCOUNT 400

DATE		EXPLANATION	POST REF.	DEBIT	CREDIT	BALANCE

MARKETING EXPENSE   ACCOUNT 510

DATE		EXPLANATION	POST REF.	DEBIT	CREDIT	BALANCE

SALARIES EXPENSE   ACCOUNT 520

DATE		EXPLANATION	POST REF.	DEBIT	CREDIT	BALANCE

P2-B4 Continued

b.

UTILITIES EXPENSE ACCOUNT 530

DATE		EXPLANATION	POST REF.	DEBIT	CREDIT	BALANCE

ACCOUNT

DATE		EXPLANATION	POST REF.	DEBIT	CREDIT	BALANCE

ACCOUNT

DATE		EXPLANATION	POST REF.	DEBIT	CREDIT	BALANCE

P2-B4   Concluded

c.

AAA Furniture Leasing

Trial Balance

February 28, 19XX

P2-B5 Clipperly Company

a.

JOURNAL

PAGE

	DATE		DESCRIPTION	POST REF.	DEBIT	CREDIT	
1							1
2							2
3							3
4							4
5							5
6							6
7							7
8							8
9							9
10							10
11							11
12							12
13							13
14							14
15							15
16							16
17							17
18							18
19							19
20							20
21							21
22							22
23							23
24							24
25							25
26							26
27							27
28							28
29							29
30							30
31							31
32							32

P2-B5 Concluded

b–c.

P2-B6 Bedford Painting

a.

Trial balance as given	2	1	0	5	0	0		1	8	1	9	0	0

P2-B6 Concluded

b.

EYH2-1 Source Documents

EYH2-1 Concluded

EYH2-2 Chart of Accounts

EYH2-2 Concluded

EYH2-3 Federal Express/The Home Depot

a–d.

EYH2-3 Concluded

EYH2-4

a–d.

EYH2-4 Concluded

CAI2-1   Carnival Corporation

CAl2-1 Concluded

P3-A1 Beta Company

a.

_____

_____

_____

_____

_____

_____

_____

_____

_____

_____

_____

_____

_____

_____

_____

_____

_____

_____

_____

_____

_____

_____

_____

_____

_____

_____

_____

_____

P3-A1 Concluded

b.

P3-A2 Butch Hallstad

a.

P3-A2 Concluded

b.

P3-A3 Fixation Enterprises

a. and c.

P3-A3 Concluded

b.

JOURNAL

PAGE

	DATE		DESCRIPTION	POST REF.	DEBIT	CREDIT	
1							1
2							2
3							3
4							4
5							5
6							6
7							7
8							8
9							9
10							10
11							11
12							12
13							13
14							14
15							15
16							16
17							17
18							18
19							19
20							20
21							21
22							22
23							23
24							24
25							25
26							26
27							27
28							28
29							29
30							30
31							31
32							32

P3-A4 Holiday Company

JOURNAL   PAGE _____

	DATE		DESCRIPTION	POST REF.	DEBIT	CREDIT	
1							1
2							2
3							3
4							4
5							5
6							6
7							7
8							8
9							9
10							10
11							11
12							12
13							13
14							14
15							15
16							16
17							17
18							18
19							19
20							20
21							21
22							22
23							23
24							24
25							25
26							26
27							27
28							28
29							29
30							30
31							31
32							32

P3-A4 Concluded

JOURNAL

PAGE

	DATE		DESCRIPTION	POST REF.	DEBIT	CREDIT	
1							1
2							2
3							3
4							4
5							5
6							6
7							7
8							8
9							9
10							10
11							11
12							12
13							13
14							14
15							15
16							16
17							17
18							18
19							19
20							20
21							21
22							22
23							23
24							24
25							25
26							26
27							27
28							28
29							29
30							30
31							31
32							32

P3-A5 Costello Company

a.

JOURNAL   PAGE _____

	DATE		DESCRIPTION	POST REF.	DEBIT	CREDIT	
1							1
2							2
3							3
4							4
5							5
6							6
7							7
8							8
9							9
10							10
11							11
12							12
13							13
14							14
15							15
16							16
17							17
18							18
19							19
20							20
21							21
22							22

c. _____

_____

_____

_____

_____

_____

_____

_____

_____

P3-A5 Costello Company

b.

Costello Company
Preparation of Adjusted Trial Balance
For the Year Ended December 31, 19XX

ACCOUNT	TRIAL BALANCE		ADJUSTMENTS		ADJUSTED TRIAL BALANCE	
	DR.	CR.	DR.	CR.	DR.	CR.
1						
2						
3						
4						
5						
6						
7						
8						
9						
10						
11						
12						
13						
14						
15						
16						
17						
18						
19						
20						
21						
22						
23						
24						
25						
26						
27						
28						
29						
30						
31						

P3-B1 Sinclair Consulting

a.

P3-B1 Concluded

b.

P3-B2 Pump It Up

a.

P3-B2 Concluded

b.

P3-B3 Southlake Enterprises

a. and c.

P3-B3 Concluded

b.

JOURNAL

PAGE

	DATE		DESCRIPTION	POST REF.	DEBIT	CREDIT	
1							1
2							2
3							3
4							4
5							5
6							6
7							7
8							8
9							9
10							10
11							11
12							12
13							13
14							14
15							15
16							16
17							17
18							18
19							19
20							20
21							21
22							22
23							23
24							24
25							25
26							26
27							27
28							28
29							29
30							30
31							31
32							32

P3-B4 Kathy's Day Care Center

JOURNAL

PAGE _____

	DATE		DESCRIPTION	POST REF.	DEBIT	CREDIT	
1							1
2							2
3							3
4							4
5							5
6							6
7							7
8							8
9							9
10							10
11							11
12							12
13							13
14							14
15							15
16							16
17							17
18							18
19							19
20							20
21							21
22							22
23							23
24							24
25							25
26							26
27							27
28							28
29							29
30							30
31							31
32							32

P3-B4 Concluded

JOURNAL

	DATE	DESCRIPTION	POST REF.	DEBIT	CREDIT	
1						1
2						2
3						3
4						4
5						5
6						6
7						7
8						8
9						9
10						10
11						11
12						12
13						13
14						14
15						15
16						16
17						17
18						18
19						19
20						20
21						21
22						22
23						23
24						24
25						25
26						26
27						27
28						28
29						29
30						30
31						31
32						32

P3-B5 Logo Company

a.

JOURNAL

PAGE

	DATE		DESCRIPTION	POST REF.	DEBIT	CREDIT	
1							1
2							2
3							3
4							4
5							5
6							6
7							7
8							8
9							9
10							10
11							11
12							12
13							13
14							14
15							15
16							16
17							17
18							18
19							19
20							20
21							21
22							22

c.

_____

_____

_____

_____

_____

_____

_____

_____

_____

P3-B5 Concluded

b.

Logo Company
Preparation of Adjusted Trial Balance
For the Year Ended December 31, 19XX

ACCOUNT	TRIAL BALANCE		ADJUSTMENTS		ADJUSTED TRIAL BALANCE	
	DR.	CR.	DR.	CR.	DR.	CR.
1						
2						
3						
4						
5						
6						
7						
8						
9						
10						
11						
12						
13						
14						
15						
16						
17						
18						
19						
20						
21						
22						
23						
24						
25						
26						
27						
28						
29						
30						
31						

EYH3-1 Accounting Periods

a.

EYH3-1 Concluded

b.

EYH3-2 Unearned Revenue

EYH3-2 Concluded

EYH3-3 Toro Company/Reader's Digest

a–e.

EYH3-3 Concluded

EYH3-4

a–e.

EYH3-4 Concluded

_____
_____
_____
_____
_____
_____
_____
_____
_____
_____
_____
_____
_____
_____
_____
_____
_____
_____
_____
_____
_____
_____
_____
_____
_____
_____
_____
_____
_____

CAI3-1   Tandy Corporation

a.

CAI3-1   Concluded

b.

P4-A1 The Fit Firm

a.

JOURNAL

PAGE

	DATE		DESCRIPTION	POST REF.	DEBIT	CREDIT	
1							1
2							2
3							3
4							4
5							5
6							6
7							7
8							8
9							9
10							10
11							11
12							12
13							13
14							14
15							15
16							16
17							17
18							18
19							19
20							20
21							21
22							22
23							23
24							24
25							25
26							26
27							27
28							28
29							29
30							30
31							31
32							32

P4-A1 Concluded

b.

Name _____

P4-A2 Columbia Repertory

a.

Columbia Repertory Theater
Work Sheet
For the Year Ended December 31, 19X6

ACCOUNT | ADJUSTED TRIAL BALANCE | INCOME STATEMENT | BALANCE SHEET

P4-A2 Continued

b.

P4-A2 Continued

b.

Columbia Repertory Theater

Income Statement

For the Year Ended December 31, 19X6

P4-A2 Continued

b.

Columbia Repertory Theater

Statement of Owner's Equity

For the Year Ended December 31, 19X6

P4-A2 Continued

b.

Columbia Repertory Theater

Balance Sheet

December 31, 19X6

P4-A2 Concluded

c.

JOURNAL

PAGE

	DATE	DESCRIPTION	POST REF.	DEBIT	CREDIT	
1						1
2						2
3						3
4						4
5						5
6						6
7						7
8						8
9						9
10						10
11						11
12						12
13						13
14						14
15						15
16						16
17						17
18						18
19						19
20						20
21						21
22						22
23						23
24						24
25						25
26						26
27						27
28						28
29						29
30						30
31						31
32						32

P4-A3 Occidental Employment

a. *The 10-column work sheet is on pages 148 and 149.*

P4-A3 Continued

a.

Occidental Employment Service

Work Sheet

For the Year Ended December 31, 19XX

ACCOUNT	TRIAL BALANCE		ADJUSTMENTS	
	DEBIT	CREDIT	DEBIT	CREDIT
1				
2				
3				
4				
5				
6				
7				
8				
9				
10				
11				
12				
13				
14				
15				
16				
17				
18				
19				
20				
21				
22				
23				
24				
25				
26				
27				
28				
29				

P4-A3 Continued

a.

	ADJUSTED TRIAL BALANCE		INCOME STATEMENT		BALANCE SHEET		
	DEBIT	CREDIT	DEBIT	CREDIT	DEBIT	CREDIT	
1							1
2							2
3							3
4							4
5							5
6							6
7							7
8							8
9							9
10							10
11							11
12							12
13							13
14							14
15							15
16							16
17							17
18							18
19							19
20							20
21							21
22							22
23							23
24							24
25							25
26							26
27							27
28							28
29							29

Page not used

P4-A3 Continued

b.

Occidental Employment Service

Income Statement

For the Year Ended December 31, 19XX

Occidental Employment Service

Statement of Owner's Equity

For the Year Ended December 31, 19XX

P4-A3 Continued

b.

Occidental Employment Service

Balance Sheet

December 31, 19XX

P4-A3 Continued

c.

JOURNAL

PAGE _____

	DATE		DESCRIPTION	POST REF.	DEBIT	CREDIT	
1							1
2							2
3							3
4							4
5							5
6							6
7							7
8							8
9							9
10							10
11							11
12							12
13							13
14							14
15							15
16							16
17							17
18							18
19							19
20							20
21							21
22							22
23							23
24							24
25							25
26							26
27							27
28							28
29							29
30							30
31							31
32							32

P4-A3 Continued

d.

JOURNAL

	DATE	DESCRIPTION	POST REF.	DEBIT	CREDIT	
1						1
2						2
3						3
4						4
5						5
6						6
7						7
8						8
9						9
10						10
11						11
12						12
13						13
14						14
15						15
16						16
17						17
18						18
19						19
20						20
21						21
22						22
23						23
24						24
25						25
26						26
27						27
28						28
29						29
30						30
31						31
32						32

P4-A3 Continued

e.

Occidental Employment Service

Post Closing Trial Balance

December 31, 19XX

P4-A3 Concluded

P4-A4 Wagner Company

Wagner Company

Balance Sheet

December 31, 19X1

P4-A4 Concluded

Wagner Company

Balance Sheet

December 31, 19X1

P4-A5 Detroit Company

a–b.

P4-A5 Concluded

P4-B1 Morton's Taxi Service

a.

JOURNAL

PAGE

	DATE	DESCRIPTION	POST REF.	DEBIT	CREDIT	
1						1
2						2
3						3
4						4
5						5
6						6
7						7
8						8
9						9
10						10
11						11
12						12
13						13
14						14
15						15
16						16
17						17
18						18
19						19
20						20
21						21
22						22
23						23
24						24
25						25
26						26
27						27
28						28
29						29
30						30
31						31
32						32

P4-B1 Concluded

JOURNAL

	DATE		DESCRIPTION	POST REF.	DEBIT	CREDIT	
1							1
2							2
3							3
4							4
5							5
6							6
7							7
8							8
9							9
10							10
11							11
12							12
13							13
14							14
15							15
16							16
17							17
18							18
19							19
20							20
21							21
22							22
23							23
24							24
25							25
26							26
27							27
28							28
29							29
30							30
31							31
32							32

P4-B2 Experts Systems Company

a.

Experts Systems Company
Work Sheet
For the Year Ended December 31, 19XX

ACCOUNT	ADJUSTED TRIAL BALANCE DR.	CR.	INCOME STATEMENT DR.	CR.	BALANCE SHEET DR.	CR.

P4-B2 Continued

b.

Expert Systems Company
Income Statement
For the Year Ended December 31, 19X6

b.

Expert Systems Company
Statement of Owner's Equity
For the Year Ended December 31, 19XX

P4-B2 Continued

b.

Expert Systems Company

Balance Sheet

December 31, 19XX

P4-B2 Concluded

c.

JOURNAL

PAGE

	DATE		DESCRIPTION	POST REF.	DEBIT	CREDIT	
1							1
2							2
3							3
4							4
5							5
6							6
7							7
8							8
9							9
10							10
11							11
12							12
13							13
14							14
15							15
16							16
17							17
18							18
19							19
20							20
21							21
22							22
23							23
24							24
25							25
26							26
27							27
28							28
29							29
30							30
31							31
32							32

P4-B3 Trimcraft Company

a. *The 10-column work sheet form is on pages 168 and 169.*

P4-B3 Continued

a.

Trimcraft Company

Work Sheet

For the Year Ended December 31, 19XX

	ACCOUNT	TRIAL BALANCE		ADJUSTMENTS	
		DEBIT	CREDIT	DEBIT	CREDIT
1					
2					
3					
4					
5					
6					
7					
8					
9					
10					
11					
12					
13					
14					
15					
16					
17					
18					
19					
20					
21					
22					
23					
24					
25					
26					
27					
28					
29					

P4-B3 Continued

a.

	ADJUSTED TRIAL BALANCE		INCOME STATEMENT		BALANCE SHEET		
	DEBIT	CREDIT	DEBIT	CREDIT	DEBIT	CREDIT	
1							1
2							2
3							3
4							4
5							5
6							6
7							7
8							8
9							9
10							10
11							11
12							12
13							13
14							14
15							15
16							16
17							17
18							18
19							19
20							20
21							21
22							22
23							23
24							24
25							25
26							26
27							27
28							28
29							29

Page not used

P4-B3 Continued

b.

Trimcraft Company

Income Statement

For the Year Ended December 31, 19XX

Trimcraft Company

Statement of Owner's Equity

For the Year Ended December 31, 19XX

P4-B3 Continued

b.

Trimcraft Company

Balance Sheet

December 31, 19XX

P4-B3 Continued

c.

		JOURNAL			PAGE	
	DATE	DESCRIPTION	POST REF.	DEBIT	CREDIT	
1						1
2						2
3						3
4						4
5						5
6						6
7						7
8						8
9						9
10						10
11						11
12						12
13						13
14						14
15						15
16						16
17						17
18						18
19						19
20						20
21						21
22						22
23						23
24						24
25						25
26						26
27						27
28						28
29						29
30						30
31						31
32						32

P4-B3 Continued

d.

JOURNAL

	DATE		DESCRIPTION	POST REF.	DEBIT	CREDIT	
1							1
2							2
3							3
4							4
5							5
6							6
7							7
8							8
9							9
10							10
11							11
12							12
13							13
14							14
15							15
16							16
17							17
18							18
19							19
20							20
21							21
22							22
23							23
24							24
25							25
26							26
27							27
28							28
29							29
30							30
31							31
32							32

P4-B3 Continued

e.

Trimcraft Company		
Post-Closing Trial Balance		
December 31, 19XX		

P4-B3 Concluded

P4-B4 Kravitz Company

Kravitz Company

Balance Sheet

December 31, 19X1

P4-B4 Concluded

Name _____

P4-B5 New York Company

a.

P4-B5   Concluded

b.

EYH4-1 Closing Experiences

EYH4-1 Concluded

EYH4-2 Unique Current Items

EYH4-2 Concluded

EYH4-3 Liquidity Differences

a.

_____

_____

_____

_____

_____

_____

_____

_____

_____

_____

_____

_____

_____

_____

_____

_____

_____

_____

_____

_____

_____

_____

_____

_____

_____

_____

_____

_____

_____

_____

_____

_____

_____

_____

EYH4-3 Concluded

b.

EYH4-4 Nike, Inc.

a–f.

EYH4-4 Concluded

EYH4-5

a–f.

EYH4-5 Concluded

EYH4-6 Apache Plastics

a–c.

EYH4-6 Concluded

EYH4-6 Concluded

CAI4-1 MCI Communications

a.

CAI4-1 Continued

CAI4-1   Continued

CAI4-1 Concluded

b.

MCI Communications

Balance Sheet

December 31, 19X0

Comprehensive Problem 1 Hamilton Company

a.

JOURNAL   PAGE

	DATE		DESCRIPTION	POST REF.	DEBIT	CREDIT	
1							1
2							2
3							3
4							4
5							5
6							6
7							7
8							8
9							9
10							10
11							11
12							12
13							13
14							14
15							15
16							16
17							17
18							18
19							19
20							20
21							21
22							22
23							23
24							24
25							25
26							26
27							27
28							28
29							29
30							30
31							31
32							32

Comprehensive Problem 1 Continued

a.

JOURNAL   PAGE

	DATE		DESCRIPTION	POST REF.	DEBIT	CREDIT	
1							1
2							2
3							3
4							4
5							5
6							6
7							7
8							8
9							9
10							10
11							11
12							12
13							13
14							14
15							15
16							16
17							17
18							18
19							19
20							20
21							21
22							22
23							23
24							24
25							25
26							26
27							27
28							28
29							29
30							30
31							31
32							32

Comprehensive Problem 1 Continued

b.

CASH   ACCOUNT 110

DATE	EXPLANATION	POST REF.	DEBIT	CREDIT	BALANCE

ACCOUNTS RECEIVABLE   ACCOUNT 120

DATE	EXPLANATION	POST REF.	DEBIT	CREDIT	BALANCE

PREPAID INSURANCE   ACCOUNT 130

DATE	EXPLANATION	POST REF.	DEBIT	CREDIT	BALANCE

OFFICE SUPPLIES   ACCOUNT 135

DATE	EXPLANATION	POST REF.	DEBIT	CREDIT	BALANCE

Comprehensive Problem 1 Continued

b.

OFFICE EQUIPMENT   ACCOUNT 140

DATE	EXPLANATION	POST REF.	DEBIT	CREDIT	BALANCE

ACCUMULATED DEPRECIATION: OFFICE EQUIPMENT   ACCOUNT 141

DATE	EXPLANATION	POST REF.	DEBIT	CREDIT	BALANCE

BUILDING   ACCOUNT 150

DATE	EXPLANATION	POST REF.	DEBIT	CREDIT	BALANCE

ACCUMULATED DEPRECIATION: BUILDING   ACCOUNT 151

DATE	EXPLANATION	POST REF.	DEBIT	CREDIT	BALANCE

Comprehensive Problem 1 Continued

b.

ACCOUNTS PAYABLE   ACCOUNT 210

DATE	EXPLANATION	POST REF.	DEBIT	CREDIT	BALANCE

WAGES PAYABLE   ACCOUNT 220

DATE	EXPLANATION	POST REF.	DEBIT	CREDIT	BALANCE

INTEREST PAYABLE   ACCOUNT 230

DATE	EXPLANATION	POST REF.	DEBIT	CREDIT	BALANCE

UTILITIES PAYABLE   ACCOUNT 240

DATE	EXPLANATION	POST REF.	DEBIT	CREDIT	BALANCE

UNEARNED SERVICE REVENUE   ACCOUNT 250

DATE	EXPLANATION	POST REF.	DEBIT	CREDIT	BALANCE

Comprehensive Problem 1 Continued

b.

LOAN PAYABLE

ACCOUNT 260

DATE	EXPLANATION	POST REF.	DEBIT	CREDIT	BALANCE

MARC NICHOLS, CAPITAL

ACCOUNT 310

DATE	EXPLANATION	POST REF.	DEBIT	CREDIT	BALANCE

MARC NICHOLS, DRAWING

ACCOUNT 320

DATE	EXPLANATION	POST REF.	DEBIT	CREDIT	BALANCE

INCOME SUMMARY

ACCOUNT 330

DATE	EXPLANATION	POST REF.	DEBIT	CREDIT	BALANCE

Comprehensive Problem 1 Continued

b.

SERVICE REVENUE

DATE	EXPLANATION	POST REF.	DEBIT	CREDIT	BALANCE

COMPUTER SERVICE EXPENSE

DATE	EXPLANATION	POST REF.	DEBIT	CREDIT	BALANCE

WAGE EXPENSE

DATE	EXPLANATION	POST REF.	DEBIT	CREDIT	BALANCE

INSURANCE EXPENSE

DATE	EXPLANATION	POST REF.	DEBIT	CREDIT	BALANCE

Comprehensive Problem 1 Continued

b.

OFFICE SUPPLIES EXPENSE

ACCOUNT 540

DATE		EXPLANATION	POST REF.	DEBIT	CREDIT	BALANCE

DEPRECIATION EXPENSE

ACCOUNT 550

DATE		EXPLANATION	POST REF.	DEBIT	CREDIT	BALANCE

UTILITIES EXPENSE

ACCOUNT 560

DATE		EXPLANATION	POST REF.	DEBIT	CREDIT	BALANCE

INTEREST EXPENSE

ACCOUNT 570

DATE		EXPLANATION	POST REF.	DEBIT	CREDIT	BALANCE

Comprehensive Problem 1 Continued

b.

MISCELLANEOUS EXPENSE

ACCOUNT 580

DATE		EXPLANATION	POST REF.	DEBIT	CREDIT	BALANCE

ACCOUNT

DATE		EXPLANATION	POST REF.	DEBIT	CREDIT	BALANCE

ACCOUNT

DATE		EXPLANATION	POST REF.	DEBIT	CREDIT	BALANCE

ACCOUNT

DATE		EXPLANATION	POST REF.	DEBIT	CREDIT	BALANCE

Comprehensive Problem 1 Continued

b.

ACCOUNT

DATE		EXPLANATION	POST REF.	DEBIT	CREDIT	BALANCE

ACCOUNT

DATE		EXPLANATION	POST REF.	DEBIT	CREDIT	BALANCE

ACCOUNT

DATE		EXPLANATION	POST REF.	DEBIT	CREDIT	BALANCE

ACCOUNT

DATE		EXPLANATION	POST REF.	DEBIT	CREDIT	BALANCE

Comprehensive Problem 1 Continued

c. *The 10-column work sheet form is on pages 208 and 209.*

Comprehensive Problem 1 Continued

c.

Hamilton Company

Work Sheet

For the Year Ended May 31, 19XX

	ACCOUNT	TRIAL BALANCE		ADJUSTMENTS		
		DEBIT	CREDIT	DEBIT	CREDIT	
1						1
2						2
3						3
4						4
5						5
6						6
7						7
8						8
9						9
10						10
11						11
12						12
13						13
14						14
15						15
16						16
17						17
18						18
19						19
20						20
21						21
22						22
23						23
24						24
25						25
26						26
27						27
28						28
29						29

Comprehensive Problem 1 Continued

c.

_____

_____

_____

	ADJUSTED TRIAL BALANCE		INCOME STATEMENT		BALANCE SHEET		
	DEBIT	CREDIT	DEBIT	CREDIT	DEBIT	CREDIT	
1							1
2							2
3							3
4							4
5							5
6							6
7							7
8							8
9							9
10							10
11							11
12							12
13							13
14							14
15							15
16							16
17							17
18							18
19							19
20							20
21							21
22							22
23							23
24							24
25							25
26							26
27							27
28							28
29							29

Page not used

Comprehensive Problem 1 Continued

d.

Hamilton Company

Income Statement

For the Month Ended May, 19XX

Comprehensive Problem 1 Continued

d.

Hamilton Company

Statement of Owner's Equity

For the Month Ended May, 19XX

Comprehensive Problem 1 Continued

d.

Hamilton Company

Balance Sheet

May 31, 19XX

Comprehensive Problem 1 Continued

e.

JOURNAL   PAGE

	DATE		DESCRIPTION	POST REF.	DEBIT	CREDIT	
1							1
2							2
3							3
4							4
5							5
6							6
7							7
8							8
9							9
10							10
11							11
12							12
13							13
14							14
15							15
16							16
17							17
18							18
19							19
20							20
21							21
22							22
23							23
24							24
25							25
26							26
27							27
28							28
29							29
30							30
31							31
32							32

Comprehensive Problem 1 Continued

f.

JOURNAL   PAGE

	DATE		DESCRIPTION	POST REF.	DEBIT	CREDIT	
1							1
2							2
3							3
4							4
5							5
6							6
7							7
8							8
9							9
10							10
11							11
12							12
13							13
14							14
15							15
16							16
17							17
18							18
19							19
20							20
21							21
22							22
23							23
24							24
25							25
26							26
27							27
28							28
29							29
30							30
31							31
32							32

Comprehensive Problem 1　Concluded

g.

Hamilton Company

Post-Closing Trial Balance

May 31, 19XX

P5-A1 Poteet and Catalina

a.

JOURNAL   PAGE

	DATE		DESCRIPTION	POST REF.	DEBIT	CREDIT	
1							1
2							2
3							3
4							4
5							5
6							6
7							7
8							8
9							9
10							10
11							11
12							12
13							13
14							14
15							15
16							16
17							17
18							18
19							19
20							20
21							21
22							22
23							23
24							24
25							25
26							26
27							27
28							28
29							29
30							30
31							31
32							32

P5-A1 Continued

b.

JOURNAL

PAGE

	DATE		DESCRIPTION	POST REF.	DEBIT	CREDIT	
1							1
2							2
3							3
4							4
5							5
6							6
7							7
8							8
9							9
10							10
11							11
12							12
13							13
14							14
15							15
16							16
17							17
18							18
19							19
20							20
21							21
22							22
23							23
24							24
25							25
26							26
27							27
28							28
29							29
30							30
31							31
32							32

P5-A1 Continued

c.

JOURNAL   PAGE

	DATE		DESCRIPTION	POST REF.	DEBIT	CREDIT	
1							1
2							2
3							3
4							4
5							5
6							6
7							7
8							8
9							9
10							10
11							11
12							12
13							13
14							14
15							15
16							16
17							17
18							18
19							19
20							20
21							21
22							22
23							23
24							24
25							25
26							26
27							27
28							28
29							29
30							30
31							31
32							32

P5-A1 Concluded

c.

P5-A2 Beth Dotterer

a.

JOURNAL   PAGE

	DATE		DESCRIPTION	POST REF.	DEBIT	CREDIT	
1							1
2							2
3							3
4							4
5							5
6							6
7							7
8							8
9							9
10							10
11							11
12							12
13							13
14							14
15							15
16							16
17							17
18							18
19							19
20							20
21							21
22							22
23							23
24							24
25							25
26							26
27							27
28							28
29							29
30							30
31							31
32							32

P5-A2 Concluded

b.

JOURNAL

	DATE	DESCRIPTION	POST REF.	DEBIT	CREDIT	
1						1
2						2
3						3
4						4
5						5
6						6
7						7
8						8
9						9
10						10
11						11
12						12
13						13
14						14
15						15
16						16
17						17
18						18
19						19
20						20
21						21
22						22

c.

P5-A3 Home Entertainment

P5-A3 Concluded

P5-A4 Juarez Corporation

a.

Juarez Corporation

Income Statement

For the Year Ended November 30, 19XX

P5-A4 Concluded

b.

P5-A5 Westbrook Enterprises

a. _____

P5-A5   Continued

b.

JOURNAL

	DATE		DESCRIPTION	POST REF.	DEBIT	CREDIT	
1							1
2							2
3							3
4							4
5							5
6							6
7							7
8							8
9							9
10							10
11							11
12							12
13							13
14							14
15							15
16							16
17							17
18							18
19							19
20							20
21							21
22							22
23							23
24							24
25							25
26							26
27							27
28							28
29							29
30							30
31							31
32							32

P5-A5 Continued

c–d.

P5-A5 Concluded

P5-A6 Wheaton Company

a. *Use the 10-column form found on pages 232 and 233.*

P5-A6 Continued

a.

Wheaton Company

Work Sheet

For the Year Ended December 31, 19XX

ACCOUNT	TRIAL BALANCE		ADJUSTMENTS	
	DEBIT	CREDIT	DEBIT	CREDIT
1				
2				
3				
4				
5				
6				
7				
8				
9				
10				
11				
12				
13				
14				
15				
16				
17				
18				
19				
20				
21				
22				
23				
24				
25				
26				
27				
28				
29				

P5-A6 Continued

a.

	ADJUSTED TRIAL BALANCE		INCOME STATEMENT		BALANCE SHEET		
	DEBIT	CREDIT	DEBIT	CREDIT	DEBIT	CREDIT	
1							1
2							2
3							3
4							4
5							5
6							6
7							7
8							8
9							9
10							10
11							11
12							12
13							13
14							14
15							15
16							16
17							17
18							18
19							19
20							20
21							21
22							22
23							23
24							24
25							25
26							26
27							27
28							28
29							29

Page not used

P5-A6 Continued

b.

Wheaton Company

Income Statement

For the Year Ended December 31, 19XX

P5-A6 Continued

b.

Wheaton Company

Statement of Owner's Equity

For the Year Ended December 31, 19XX

P5-A6 Continued

b.

Wheaton Company

Balance Sheet

December 31, 19XX

P5-A6 Continued

c.

JOURNAL

PAGE

	DATE		DESCRIPTION	POST REF.	DEBIT	CREDIT	
1							1
2							2
3							3
4							4
5							5
6							6
7							7
8							8
9							9
10							10
11							11
12							12
13							13
14							14
15							15
16							16
17							17
18							18
19							19
20							20
21							21
22							22
23							23
24							24
25							25
26							26
27							27
28							28
29							29
30							30
31							31
32							32

P5-A6 Continued

d.

JOURNAL   PAGE

	DATE		DESCRIPTION	POST REF.	DEBIT	CREDIT	
1							1
2							2
3							3
4							4
5							5
6							6
7							7
8							8
9							9
10							10
11							11
12							12
13							13
14							14
15							15
16							16
17							17
18							18
19							19
20							20
21							21
22							22
23							23
24							24
25							25
26							26
27							27
28							28
29							29
30							30
31							31
32							32

P5-A6 Concluded

JOURNAL

	DATE	DESCRIPTION	POST REF.	DEBIT	CREDIT	
1						1
2						2
3						3
4						4
5						5
6						6
7						7
8						8
9						9
10						10
11						11
12						12
13						13
14						14
15						15
16						16
17						17
18						18
19						19
20						20
21						21
22						22
23						23
24						24
25						25
26						26
27						27
28						28
29						29
30						30
31						31
32						32

Name _____

P5-B1 Patrick Company

JOURNAL   PAGE _____

	DATE	DESCRIPTION	POST REF.	DEBIT	CREDIT
1					
2					
3					
4					
5					
6					
7					
8					
9					
10					
11					
12					
13					
14					
15					
16					
17					
18					
19					
20					
21					
22					
23					
24					
25					
26					
27					
28					
29					
30					
31					
32					

P5-B1 Concluded

JOURNAL

PAGE

	DATE	DESCRIPTION	POST REF.	DEBIT	CREDIT	
1						1
2						2
3						3
4						4
5						5
6						6
7						7
8						8
9						9
10						10
11						11
12						12
13						13
14						14
15						15
16						16
17						17
18						18
19						19
20						20
21						21
22						22
23						23
24						24
25						25
26						26
27						27
28						28
29						29
30						30
31						31
32						32

P5-B2 Beautiful Face

a.

JOURNAL   PAGE _____

	DATE		DESCRIPTION	POST REF.	DEBIT	CREDIT	
1							1
2							2
3							3
4							4
5							5
6							6
7							7
8							8
9							9
10							10
11							11
12							12
13							13
14							14
15							15
16							16
17							17
18							18
19							19
20							20
21							21
22							22
23							23
24							24
25							25
26							26
27							27
28							28
29							29
30							30
31							31
32							32

P5-B2 Concluded

b.

JOURNAL

	DATE		DESCRIPTION	POST REF.	DEBIT	CREDIT	
1							1
2							2
3							3
4							4
5							5
6							6
7							7
8							8
9							9
10							10
11							11
12							12
13							13
14							14
15							15
16							16
17							17
18							18
19							19
20							20
21							21
22							22
23							23
24							24
25							25
26							26
27							27
28							28
29							29
30							30
31							31
32							32

P5-B3 Second Time Around

P5-B3 Concluded

P5-B4 Hanson Corporation

a.

Hanson Corporation

Income Statement

For the Year Ended September 30, 19X4

P5-B4   Concluded

b.

P5-B5 Hidden Valley, Inc.

a.

_____
_____
_____
_____
_____
_____
_____
_____
_____
_____
_____

b.

JOURNAL   PAGE

	DATE		DESCRIPTION	POST REF.	DEBIT	CREDIT	
1							1
2							2
3							3
4							4
5							5
6							6
7							7
8							8
9							9
10							10
11							11
12							12
13							13
14							14
15							15
16							16
17							17
18							18
19							19
20							20

P5-B5 Concluded

c–d.

P5-B6 Phoenix Appliance

a. *Use the 10-column form found on pages 252 and 253.*

P5-B6 Continued

a.

Phoenix Appliance

Work Sheet

For the Year Ended December 31, 19XX

	ACCOUNT	TRIAL BALANCE		ADJUSTMENTS		
		DEBIT	CREDIT	DEBIT	CREDIT	
1						1
2						2
3						3
4						4
5						5
6						6
7						7
8						8
9						9
10						10
11						11
12						12
13						13
14						14
15						15
16						16
17						17
18						18
19						19
20						20
21						21
22						22
23						23
24						24
25						25
26						26
27						27
28						28
29						29

P5-B6 Continued

a.

_____

	ADJUSTED TRIAL BALANCE		INCOME STATEMENT		BALANCE SHEET		
	DEBIT	CREDIT	DEBIT	CREDIT	DEBIT	CREDIT	
1							1
2							2
3							3
4							4
5							5
6							6
7							7
8							8
9							9
10							10
11							11
12							12
13							13
14							14
15							15
16							16
17							17
18							18
19							19
20							20
21							21
22							22
23							23
24							24
25							25
26							26
27							27
28							28
29							29

Page not used

P5-B6 Continued

b.

Phoenix Appliance

Income Statement

For the Year Ended December 31, 19XX

P5-B6 Continued

b.

Phoenix Appliance

Statement of Owner's Equity

For the Year Ended December 31, 19XX

P5-B6 Continued

b.

Phoenix Appliance

Balance Sheet

December 31, 19XX

P5-B6 Continued

c.

JOURNAL

	DATE	DESCRIPTION	POST REF.	DEBIT	CREDIT	
1						1
2						2
3						3
4						4
5						5
6						6
7						7
8						8
9						9
10						10
11						11
12						12
13						13
14						14
15						15
16						16
17						17
18						18
19						19
20						20
21						21
22						22
23						23
24						24
25						25
26						26
27						27
28						28
29						29
30						30
31						31
32						32

P5-B6 Continued

d.

JOURNAL   PAGE

	DATE		DESCRIPTION	POST REF.	DEBIT	CREDIT	
1							1
2							2
3							3
4							4
5							5
6							6
7							7
8							8
9							9
10							10
11							11
12							12
13							13
14							14
15							15
16							16
17							17
18							18
19							19
20							20
21							21
22							22
23							23
24							24
25							25
26							26
27							27
28							28
29							29
30							30
31							31
32							32

P5-B6 Concluded

JOURNAL

	DATE		DESCRIPTION	POST REF.	DEBIT	CREDIT	
1							1
2							2
3							3
4							4
5							5
6							6
7							7
8							8
9							9
10							10
11							11
12							12
13							13
14							14
15							15
16							16
17							17
18							18
19							19
20							20
21							21
22							22
23							23
24							24
25							25
26							26
27							27
28							28
29							29
30							30
31							31
32							32

P5-B6 Concluded

EYH5-1 Sales Returns

EYH5-1 Concluded

EYH5-2 Cash Discounts

EYH5-2 Concluded

EYH5-3 Merchandising Systems

EYH5-3 Concluded

EYH5-4 Nordstrom, Inc./Office Depot Inc.

a–d.

EYH5-4 Concluded

EYH5-5

a–d.

EYH5-5 Concluded

EYH5-6   Paul Davis

a–e.

EYH5-6 Concluded

CAl5-1 Woolworth Corp.

CAI5-1 Concluded

P6-A1 Haskell Company

a–d.

P6-A1 Concluded

P6-A2 Pro Auto Supply

a–c.

P6-A2 Concluded

P6-A3 Express Boat Repair

a.

JOURNAL   PAGE

	DATE		DESCRIPTION	POST REF.	DEBIT	CREDIT	
1							1
2							2
3							3
4							4
5							5
6							6
7							7
8							8
9							9
10							10
11							11
12							12
13							13
14							14
15							15
16							16
17							17
18							18
19							19
20							20
21							21
22							22
23							23
24							24
25							25
26							26
27							27
28							28
29							29
30							30
31							31
32							32

P6-A3 Continued

b.

CASH   ACCOUNT 101

DATE	EXPLANATION	POST REF.	DEBIT	CREDIT	BALANCE

OFFICE SUPPLIES   ACCOUNT 120

DATE	EXPLANATION	POST REF.	DEBIT	CREDIT	BALANCE

MACHINERY   ACCOUNT130

DATE	EXPLANATION	POST REF.	DEBIT	CREDIT	BALANCE

P6-A3 Continued

b.

ACCUMULATED DEPRECIATION ACCOUNT 131

DATE	EXPLANATION	POST REF.	DEBIT	CREDIT	BALANCE

UTILITIES PAYABLE ACCOUNT 200

DATE	EXPLANATION	POST REF.	DEBIT	CREDIT	BALANCE

INTEREST PAYABLE ACCOUNT 210

DATE	EXPLANATION	POST REF.	DEBIT	CREDIT	BALANCE

P6-A3 Continued

b.

LOAN PAYABLE   ACCOUNT 220

DATE	EXPLANATION	POST REF.	DEBIT	CREDIT	BALANCE

KEITH PRICE, CAPITAL   ACCOUNT 310

DATE	EXPLANATION	POST REF.	DEBIT	CREDIT	BALANCE

KEITH PRICE, DRAWING   ACCOUNT 320

DATE	EXPLANATION	POST REF.	DEBIT	CREDIT	BALANCE

P6-A3 Continued

b.

SERVICE REVENUE   ACCOUNT 410

DATE		EXPLANATION	POST REF.	DEBIT	CREDIT	BALANCE

OFFICE SUPPLIES EXPENSE   ACCOUNT 500

DATE		EXPLANATION	POST REF.	DEBIT	CREDIT	BALANCE

ADVERTISING EXPENSE   ACCOUNT 510

DATE		EXPLANATION	POST REF.	DEBIT	CREDIT	BALANCE

P6-A3 Continued

b.

UTILITIES EXPENSE

ACCOUNT 520

DATE	EXPLANATION	POST REF.	DEBIT	CREDIT	BALANCE

RENT EXPENSE

ACCOUNT 530

DATE	EXPLANATION	POST REF.	DEBIT	CREDIT	BALANCE

DEPRECIATION EXPENSE

ACCOUNT 540

DATE	EXPLANATION	POST REF.	DEBIT	CREDIT	BALANCE

P6-A3 Continued

b.

INTEREST EXPENSE _____ ACCOUNT 550

DATE	EXPLANATION	POST REF.	DEBIT	CREDIT	BALANCE

ACCOUNT

DATE	EXPLANATION	POST REF.	DEBIT	CREDIT	BALANCE

ACCOUNT

DATE	EXPLANATION	POST REF.	DEBIT	CREDIT	BALANCE

P6-A3 Continued

b.

Express Boat Repair

Adjusted Trial Balance

January 31, 19X5

P6-A3 Continued

b.

Express Boat Repair

Income Statement

For the Month Ended January 31, 19X5

Express Boat Repair

Statement of Owner's Equity

For the Month Ended January 31, 19X5

P6-A3 Concluded

b.

Express Boat Repair

Balance Sheet

January 31, 19X5

P6-A4 Control Evaluation

a–f.

P6-A4 Concluded

P6-A5 First Church

P6-A5 Concluded

P6-B1 Bismarck Company

a–d.

P6-B1　Concluded

P6-B2 Austin Products

a–d.

P6-B2 Concluded

P6-B3 Tri Cities Automotive

a.

JOURNAL   PAGE

	DATE		DESCRIPTION	POST REF.	DEBIT	CREDIT	
1							1
2							2
3							3
4							4
5							5
6							6
7							7
8							8
9							9
10							10
11							11
12							12
13							13
14							14
15							15
16							16
17							17
18							18
19							19
20							20
21							21
22							22
23							23
24							24
25							25
26							26
27							27
28							28
29							29
30							30
31							31
32							32

P6-B3 Continued

a.

JOURNAL

	DATE		DESCRIPTION	POST REF.	DEBIT	CREDIT	
1							1
2							2
3							3
4							4
5							5
6							6
7							7
8							8
9							9
10							10
11							11
12							12
13							13
14							14
15							15
16							16
17							17
18							18
19							19
20							20
21							21
22							22
23							23
24							24
25							25
26							26
27							27
28							28
29							29
30							30
31							31
32							32

P6-B3 Continued

b.

CASH

DATE	EXPLANATION	POST REF.	DEBIT	CREDIT	BALANCE

SUPPLIES

DATE	EXPLANATION	POST REF.	DEBIT	CREDIT	BALANCE

EQUIPMENT

DATE	EXPLANATION	POST REF.	DEBIT	CREDIT	BALANCE

P6-B3 Continued

b.

ACCUMULATED DEPRECIATION   ACCOUNT 121

DATE		EXPLANATION	POST REF.	DEBIT	CREDIT	BALANCE

UTILITIES PAYABLE   ACCOUNT 200

DATE		EXPLANATION	POST REF.	DEBIT	CREDIT	BALANCE

LOAN PAYABLE   ACCOUNT 210

DATE		EXPLANATION	POST REF.	DEBIT	CREDIT	BALANCE

P6-B3 Continued

b.

INTEREST PAYABLE   ACCOUNT 220

DATE	EXPLANATION	POST REF.	DEBIT	CREDIT	BALANCE

BUDDY HAWKINS, CAPITAL   ACCOUNT 300

DATE	EXPLANATION	POST REF.	DEBIT	CREDIT	BALANCE

BUDDY HAWKINS, DRAWING   ACCOUNT 310

DATE	EXPLANATION	POST REF.	DEBIT	CREDIT	BALANCE

P6-B3 Continued

b.

SERVICE REVENUE

ACCOUNT 400

DATE		EXPLANATION	POST REF.	DEBIT	CREDIT	BALANCE

SUPPLIES EXPENSE

ACCOUNT 500

DATE		EXPLANATION	POST REF.	DEBIT	CREDIT	BALANCE

INSURANCE EXPENSE

ACCOUNT 510

DATE		EXPLANATION	POST REF.	DEBIT	CREDIT	BALANCE

P6-B3 Continued

b.

RENT EXPENSE

DATE	EXPLANATION	POST REF.	DEBIT	CREDIT	BALANCE

UTILITIES EXPENSE

DATE	EXPLANATION	POST REF.	DEBIT	CREDIT	BALANCE

DEPRECIATION EXPENSE

DATE	EXPLANATION	POST REF.	DEBIT	CREDIT	BALANCE

P6-B3 Continued

b.

INTEREST EXPENSE   ACCOUNT 550

DATE	EXPLANATION	POST REF.	DEBIT	CREDIT	BALANCE

ACCOUNT

DATE	EXPLANATION	POST REF.	DEBIT	CREDIT	BALANCE

ACCOUNT

DATE	EXPLANATION	POST REF.	DEBIT	CREDIT	BALANCE

P6-B3 Continued

b.

	Tri Cities Automotive

Adjusted Trial Balance

January 31, 19X3

P6-B3 Continued

b.

Tri Cities Automotive

Income Statement

For the Month Ended January 31, 19X3

Name _____

P6-B3 Continued

b.

Tri Cities Automotive

Statement of Owner's Equity

For the Month Ended January 31, 19X3

P6-B3 Concluded

b.

Tri Cities Automotive

Balance Sheet

January 31, 19X3

P6-B4 Control Evaluation

a–f.

_____

_____

_____

_____

_____

_____

_____

_____

_____

_____

_____

_____

_____

_____

_____

_____

_____

_____

_____

_____

_____

_____

_____

_____

_____

_____

_____

_____

_____

_____

_____

_____

_____

P6-B4 Concluded

P6-B5 Jimmy's

a.

_____

_____

_____

_____

_____

_____

_____

_____

_____

_____

_____

_____

_____

_____

_____

_____

_____

_____

_____

_____

_____

_____

_____

_____

_____

_____

_____

_____

_____

_____

_____

P6-B5 Concluded

b.

EYH6-1 Accounting Software Packages

EYHB6-1 Concluded

EYH6-2 Internal Control and CPAs

EYH6-2 Concluded

EYH6-3 Computer Crime

EYH6-3 Concluded

EYH6-4 Eagle Engineering

a.

EYH6-4 Concluded

b.

	Engineering Services	Accounting & Finance	Marketing
Items of equipment owned			
Slow-paying accounts			
Budget vs. actual year-to-date expenditures			
Worker's compensation claims			
Construction costs by job			
Analysis of fringe benefits			
New contracts signed			
Entertainment expenditures			
Unemployment rates and Gross Domestic Product (GDP) data			

CAI6-1   United Technologies

CAI6-1 Concluded

P7-A1 Maverick Foods

a–d.

_____

_____

_____

_____

_____

_____

_____

_____

_____

_____

_____

_____

_____

_____

_____

_____

_____

_____

_____

_____

_____

_____

_____

_____

_____

_____

_____

_____

_____

P7-A1 Concluded

P7-A2 Jan Clayton

a–i.

P7-A2 Concluded

P7-A3 Garjullo Canning

P7-A3 Concluded

P7-B1 Libby Co.

a–d.

P7-B1 Concluded

Name _____

P7-B2 Skip Dowdy

a–i.

P7-B2 Concluded

P7-B3 Tacoma Paper

P7-B3 Concluded

EYH7-1 Quality of Earnings

EYH7-1   Concluded

EYH7-2 Annual Reports

EYH7-2 Concluded

EYH7-3 Letter to Stockholders

EYH7-3 Concluded

CAI7-1 ATP Industries

CAI7-1 Concluded

P8-A1 Performance Auto Repair

a–c.

P8-A1 Concluded

P8-A2 Eason Company

a.

Eason Company

Bank Reconciliation

December 31, 19XX

P8-A2 Concluded

b.

JOURNAL   PAGE

	DATE		DESCRIPTION	POST REF.	DEBIT		CREDIT		
1									1
2									2
3									3
4									4
5									5
6									6
7									7
8									8
9									9
10									10
11									11
12									12
13									13
14									14
15									15
16									16
17									17
18									18
19									19
20									20

c.

_____

_____

_____

_____

_____

_____

_____

_____

_____

_____

_____

_____

P8-A3 The Union Company

a.

The Union Company

Bank Reconciliation

May 31, 19XX

P8-A3 Concluded

b.

JOURNAL

PAGE _____

	DATE		DESCRIPTION	POST REF.	DEBIT	CREDIT	
1							1
2							2
3							3
4							4
5							5
6							6
7							7
8							8
9							9
10							10
11							11
12							12
13							13
14							14
15							15
16							16
17							17
18							18
19							19
20							20
21							21
22							22
23							23
24							24
25							25
26							26
27							27
28							28
29							29
30							30
31							31
32							32

P8-A4 United Enterprises

a.

JOURNAL

PAGE _____

	DATE		DESCRIPTION	POST REF.	DEBIT	CREDIT	
1							1
2							2
3							3
4							4
5							5
6							6
7							7
8							8
9							9
10							10
11							11
12							12
13							13
14							14
15							15
16							16
17							17
18							18
19							19
20							20
21							21
22							22
23							23
24							24
25							25
26							26
27							27
28							28
29							29
30							30
31							31
32							32

P8-A4 Concluded

b.

P8-A5 Redford Company

a.

			JOURNAL			PAGE		
	DATE		DESCRIPTION	POST REF.	DEBIT	CREDIT		
1								1
2								2
3								3
4								4
5								5
6								6
7								7
8								8
9								9
10								10
11								11
12								12
13								13
14								14

b.

			JOURNAL			PAGE		
	DATE		DESCRIPTION	POST REF.	DEBIT	CREDIT		
1								1
2								2
3								3
4								4
5								5
6								6
7								7
8								8
9								9
10								10
11								11
12								12
13								13
14								14

P8-A5 Concluded

c–e.

JOURNAL

PAGE

	DATE		DESCRIPTION	POST REF.	DEBIT	CREDIT	
1							1
2							2
3							3
4							4
5							5
6							6
7							7
8							8
9							9
10							10
11							11
12							12
13							13
14							14
15							15
16							16
17							17
18							18
19							19
20							20
21							21
22							22
23							23
24							24
25							25
26							26
27							27
28							28
29							29
30							30
31							31
32							32

P8-B1 Gateway, Inc.

a.

P8-B1   Concluded

b.

P8-B2 Elshazly Company

a.

Elshazly Company

Bank Reconciliation

October 31, 19XX

P8-B2 Concluded

b.

JOURNAL   PAGE

	DATE		DESCRIPTION	POST REF.	DEBIT	CREDIT	
1							1
2							2
3							3
4							4
5							5
6							6
7							7
8							8
9							9
10							10
11							11
12							12
13							13
14							14
15							15
16							16
17							17
18							18
19							19
20							20

c.

P8-B3 Whitlow Corporation

a.

Whitlow Corporation							
Bank Reconciliation							
September 30, 19XX							

P8-B3   Concluded

b.

JOURNAL

	DATE		DESCRIPTION	POST REF.	DEBIT	CREDIT	
1							1
2							2
3							3
4							4
5							5
6							6
7							7
8							8
9							9
10							10
11							11
12							12
13							13
14							14
15							15
16							16
17							17
18							18
19							19
20							20
21							21
22							22
23							23
24							24
25							25
26							26
27							27
28							28
29							29
30							30
31							31
32							32

P8-B4 Dekalb Enterprises

a.

JOURNAL

	DATE		DESCRIPTION	POST REF.	DEBIT	CREDIT	
1							1
2							2
3							3
4							4
5							5
6							6
7							7
8							8
9							9
10							10
11							11
12							12
13							13
14							14
15							15
16							16
17							17
18							18
19							19
20							20
21							21
22							22
23							23
24							24
25							25
26							26
27							27
28							28
29							29
30							30
31							31
32							32

P8-B4 Concluded

b.

P8-B5 James Company

a–b.

JOURNAL

	DATE		DESCRIPTION	POST REF.	DEBIT	CREDIT	
1							1
2							2
3							3
4							4
5							5
6							6
7							7
8							8
9							9
10							10
11							11
12							12
13							13
14							14
15							15
16							16
17							17
18							18
19							19
20							20
21							21
22							22
23							23
24							24
25							25
26							26
27							27
28							28
29							29
30							30
31							31
32							32

P8-B5 Concluded

c–e.

JOURNAL

PAGE

	DATE		DESCRIPTION	POST REF.	DEBIT	CREDIT	
1							1
2							2
3							3
4							4
5							5
6							6
7							7
8							8
9							9
10							10
11							11
12							12
13							13
14							14
15							15
16							16
17							17
18							18
19							19
20							20
21							21
22							22
23							23
24							24
25							25
26							26
27							27
28							28
29							29
30							30
31							31
32							32

EYH8-1   Personal Cash Budget

a.

EYH8-1 Concluded

b.

EYH8-2 Cash Embezzlement

EYH8-2 Concluded

EYH8-3 Reconciling Your Account

a–c.

EYH8-3 Concluded

EYH8-4 Visiting a Broker

a.

EYH8-4 Concluded

b.

EYH8-5 Freeport Foods

a–d.

EYH8-5 Concluded

CAI8-1 Dun & Bradstreet

CAI8-1 Concluded

P9-A1 Hardaway Company

a–c.

JOURNAL

	DATE		DESCRIPTION	POST REF.	DEBIT	CREDIT	
1							1
2							2
3							3
4							4
5							5
6							6
7							7
8							8
9							9
10							10
11							11
12							12
13							13
14							14
15							15
16							16
17							17
18							18
19							19
20							20
21							21
22							22
23							23
24							24
25							25
26							26
27							27
28							28
29							29
30							30
31							31
32							32

P9-A1 Concluded

JOURNAL

PAGE

	DATE		DESCRIPTION	POST REF.	DEBIT	CREDIT	
1							1
2							2
3							3
4							4
5							5
6							6
7							7
8							8
9							9
10							10
11							11
12							12
13							13
14							14
15							15
16							16
17							17
18							18
19							19
20							20
21							21
22							22
23							23
24							24
25							25
26							26
27							27
28							28
29							29
30							30
31							31
32							32

P9-A2 Tempe Company

a–b.

JOURNAL   PAGE

	DATE		DESCRIPTION	POST REF.	DEBIT	CREDIT	
1							1
2							2
3							3
4							4
5							5
6							6
7							7
8							8
9							9
10							10
11							11
12							12
13							13
14							14
15							15
16							16
17							17
18							18
19							19
20							20
21							21
22							22
23							23
24							24
25							25
26							26
27							27
28							28
29							29
30							30
31							31
32							32

P9-A2 Concluded

c.

JOURNAL   PAGE _____

	DATE		DESCRIPTION	POST REF.	DEBIT	CREDIT	
1							1
2							2
3							3
4							4
5							5
6							6
7							7
8							8
9							9
10							10
11							11
12							12
13							13
14							14
15							15
16							16
17							17
18							18
19							19

d.

P9-A3 Phone Merchandising

a–d.

P9-A3 Concluded

P9-A4 Kenwood Company

a. and c.

JOURNAL

PAGE _____

	DATE		DESCRIPTION	POST REF.	DEBIT	CREDIT	
1							1
2							2
3							3
4							4
5							5
6							6
7							7
8							8
9							9
10							10
11							11
12							12
13							13
14							14
15							15
16							16
17							17
18							18
19							19
20							20
21							21
22							22
23							23
24							24
25							25
26							26
27							27
28							28
29							29
30							30
31							31
32							32

P9-A4 Concluded

a. and c.

JOURNAL   PAGE

	DATE		DESCRIPTION	POST REF.	DEBIT	CREDIT	
1							1
2							2
3							3
4							4
5							5
6							6
7							7
8							8
9							9
10							10
11							11
12							12
13							13
14							14
15							15
16							16
17							17
18							18
19							19
20							20
21							21
22							22

b.

P9-A5 Cicero Company

a.

JOURNAL   PAGE

	DATE		DESCRIPTION	POST REF.	DEBIT	CREDIT	
1							1
2							2
3							3
4							4
5							5
6							6
7							7
8							8
9							9
10							10
11							11
12							12
13							13
14							14
15							15
16							16
17							17
18							18
19							19
20							20
21							21
22							22
23							23
24							24
25							25
26							26
27							27
28							28
29							29
30							30
31							31
32							32

P9-A5 Cicero Company

P9-A5 Concluded

b–c.

_____
_____
_____
_____
_____
_____
_____
_____
_____
_____
_____
_____
_____

c–d.

JOURNAL   PAGE _____

	DATE	DESCRIPTION	POST REF.	DEBIT	CREDIT	
1						1
2						2
3						3
4						4
5						5
6						6
7						7
8						8
9						9
10						10
11						11
12						12
13						13
14						14
15						15
16						16
17						17

P9-B1 Yelland Company

a–c.

JOURNAL   PAGE

	DATE		DESCRIPTION	POST REF.	DEBIT	CREDIT	
1							1
2							2
3							3
4							4
5							5
6							6
7							7
8							8
9							9
10							10
11							11
12							12
13							13
14							14
15							15
16							16
17							17
18							18
19							19
20							20
21							21
22							22
23							23
24							24
25							25
26							26
27							27
28							28
29							29
30							30
31							31
32							32

P9-B1 Concluded

JOURNAL

	DATE	DESCRIPTION	POST REF.	DEBIT	CREDIT	
1						1
2						2
3						3
4						4
5						5
6						6
7						7
8						8
9						9
10						10
11						11
12						12
13						13
14						14

d.

Name _____

P9-B2 Huffy Company

a–b.

JOURNAL   PAGE

	DATE		DESCRIPTION	POST REF.	DEBIT	CREDIT	
1							1
2							2
3							3
4							4
5							5
6							6
7							7
8							8
9							9
10							10
11							11
12							12
13							13
14							14
15							15
16							16
17							17
18							18
19							19
20							20
21							21
22							22
23							23
24							24
25							25
26							26
27							27
28							28
29							29
30							30
31							31
32							32

P9-B2 Concluded

c.

JOURNAL

PAGE

	DATE		DESCRIPTION	POST REF.	DEBIT	CREDIT	
1							1
2							2
3							3
4							4
5							5
6							6
7							7
8							8
9							9
10							10
11							11
12							12
13							13
14							14
15							15
16							16
17							17
18							18
19							19

d.

P9-B3 Sonic Sound

a–d.

_____

_____

_____

_____

_____

_____

_____

_____

_____

_____

_____

_____

_____

_____

_____

_____

_____

_____

_____

_____

_____

_____

_____

_____

_____

_____

_____

_____

_____

_____

_____

P9-B3 Concluded

P9-B4 Letterman Company

a.

JOURNAL   PAGE

	DATE		DESCRIPTION	POST REF.	DEBIT	CREDIT	
1							1
2							2
3							3
4							4
5							5
6							6
7							7
8							8
9							9
10							10
11							11
12							12
13							13
14							14
15							15
16							16
17							17
18							18
19							19
20							20
21							21
22							22
23							23
24							24
25							25
26							26
27							27
28							28
29							29
30							30
31							31
32							32

P9-B4 Letterman Company

P9-B4   Concluded

b–c.

P9-B5 Smith Trucking

a–b.

P9-B5 Concluded

c.

JOURNAL

	DATE	DESCRIPTION	POST REF.	DEBIT	CREDIT	
1						1
2						2
3						3
4						4
5						5
6						6
7						7
8						8
9						9
10						10
11						11
12						12
13						13
14						14
15						15
16						16
17						17
18						18
19						19
20						20
21						21
22						22

d.

EYH9-1 Credit Reporting

a.

EYH9-1 Concluded

b.

EYH9-2 Uncollectible Accounts

EYH9-2 Concluded

Name _____

EYH9-3 Student Loans

EYH9-3 Concluded

EYH9-4 Ralston Purina/Hershey Foods

a–d.

EYH9-4 Concluded

EYH9-5 May Department Stores

a–d.

EYH9-5 Concluded

EYH9-6 Alomar Tire Company

a–d.

EYH9-6 Concluded

CAI9-1 Dun & Bradstreet

CAl9-1 Concluded

P10-A1   Diamond Company

a.

Diamond Company

Corrected Income Statement

For the Year Ended December 31, 19X1

P10-A1 Concluded

a.

Diamond Company

Corrected Income Statement

For the Year Ended December 31, 19X2

b.

P10-A2   Alpine Snowboards

a–b.

P10-A2 Concluded

P10-A3 Tall Pine Nursery

a.

P10-A3 Concluded

b.

_____
_____
_____
_____
_____
_____
_____
_____
_____
_____
_____
_____
_____
_____
_____
_____
_____
_____
_____
_____
_____
_____
_____

c.

JOURNAL

PAGE

	DATE	DESCRIPTION	POST REF.	DEBIT	CREDIT	
1						1
2						2
3						3
4						4
5						5
6						6
7						7
8						8
9						9
10						10

P10-A4 Sunset Products

a–c.

P10-A4 Concluded

P10-A5 Sarah Anne's

a–d.

_____

_____

_____

_____

_____

_____

_____

_____

_____

_____

_____

_____

_____

_____

_____

_____

_____

_____

_____

_____

_____

_____

_____

_____

_____

_____

_____

_____

_____

_____

_____

_____

P10-A5 Concluded

P10-A6 Schaber Company

a.

Heart Monitor

Date	Purchases	Sales	Balance
5/1			100 @ $6,800

P10-A6 Concluded

b.

	DATE		DESCRIPTION	POST REF.	DEBIT	CREDIT	
1							1
2							2
3							3
4							4
5							5
6							6
7							7
8							8
9							9
10							10
11							11
12							12
13							13
14							14
15							15
16							16
17							17
18							18
19							19
20							20
21							21

JOURNAL   PAGE

c.

P10-A7 Schaber Company

a.

Heart Monitor

Date	Purchases	Sales	Balance
5/1			100 @ $6,800

P10-A7 Continued

b.

Heart Monitor

Date	Purchases	Sales	Balance
5/1			100 @ $6,800

P10-A7 Continued

Date	Purchases	Sales	Balance

P10-A7 Concluded

P10-B1 Maxum Company

a.

Maxum Company

Corrected Income Statement

For the Year Ended December 31, 19X4

P10-B1 Concluded

a.

	Maxum Company
	Corrected Income Statement
	For the Year Ended December 31, 19X5

b.

Name _____

P10-B2 Roller Blade

a–b.

P10-B2 Concluded

P10-B3 Davenport Opticians

a–b.

P10-B3 Concluded

_____

c.

JOURNAL   PAGE

	DATE		DESCRIPTION	POST REF.	DEBIT	CREDIT	
1							1
2							2
3							3
4							4
5							5
6							6
7							7
8							8
9							9
10							10

P10-B4 Fresno Home Video

a–c.

P10-B4   Concluded

P10-B5   Pro Stop

a–c.

P10-B5 Concluded

P10-B6 Classrooms, Etc.

a.

U. S. Map

Date	Purchases	Sales	Balance
10/1			40 @ $68

P10-B6　Concluded

b.

JOURNAL

PAGE

	DATE	DESCRIPTION	POST REF.	DEBIT	CREDIT	
1						1
2						2
3						3
4						4
5						5
6						6
7						7
8						8
9						9
10						10
11						11
12						12
13						13
14						14
15						15
16						16
17						17
18						18
19						19
20						20
21						21

c.

P10-B7 Classrooms, Etc.

a.

U. S. Map

Date	Purchases	Sales	Balance
10/1			40 @ $68

P10-B7 Continued

b.

U. S. Map

Date	Purchases	Sales	Balance
10/1			40 @ $68

P10-B7 Continued

Date	Purchases	Sales	Balance

P10-B7 Concluded

EYH10-1 Inventory Methods

a.

EYH10-1   Concluded

b.

EYH10-2 Lower of Cost or Market

EYH10-2 Concluded

EYH10-3 Inventory Turnover

EYH10-3 Concluded

EYH10-4   J. M. Smucker Company

a–d.

EYH10-4 Concluded

EYH10-5

a–d.

EYH10-5 Concluded

EYH10-6 The Biscayne Company

a–d.

EYH10-6 Concluded

CAI10-1 Goodyear Tire and Rubber

CAI10-1 Concluded

P11-A1 Steinberg Company

P11-A1 Concluded

P11-A2 Cheryl Livingston

Date	Land	Land Improvements	Building	Furniture & Equipment
	$	$	$	$

P11-A2 Concluded

P11-A3 Aussie Imports

a–c.

P11-A3 Concluded

P11-A4 Executive Lift

a–b.

P11-A4 Concluded

Name _____

P11-A5 Epson Company

P11-A5 Concluded

P11-A6 Bubba Clark

a.

P11-A6 Concluded

b.

JOURNAL

	DATE	DESCRIPTION	POST REF.	DEBIT	CREDIT	
1						1
2						2
3						3
4						4
5						5
6						6
7						7
8						8
9						9
10						10
11						11
12						12
13						13
14						14

c.

P11-B1 Jacksonville Company

a–b.

P11-B1 Jacksonville Company

P11-B1 Concluded

Name _____

P11-B2 Sabre Company

a.

Date	Land	Land Improvements	Building	Equipment
	$	$	$	$

P11-B2   Concluded

P11-B3 Furrell Company

a–c.

P11-B3 Concluded

P11-B4 Empire Treats, Inc.

a.

P11-B4 Concluded

b.

P11-B5 Sheppard Exports

a–c.

P11-B5 Concluded

P11-B6 Mike Miller

a.

P11-B6 Concluded

b.

c.

JOURNAL   PAGE _____

	DATE	DESCRIPTION	POST REF.	DEBIT	CREDIT	
1						1
2						2
3						3
4						4
5						5
6						6
7						7
8						8
9						9
10						10
11						11
12						12
13						13
14						14

EYH11-1   Service Life Variation

a–c.

_____

_____

_____

_____

_____

_____

_____

_____

_____

_____

_____

_____

_____

_____

_____

_____

_____

_____

_____

_____

_____

_____

_____

_____

_____

_____

_____

_____

_____

_____

_____

_____

EYH11-1 Concluded

EYH11-2 Service Life Revision

EYH11-2 Concluded

EYH11-3 Popularity of Leases

a–d.

EYH11-3 Concluded

EYH11-4 Rubbermaid Incorporated/Sherwin Williams

a–e.

EYH11-4 Concluded

EYH11-5

a–e.

EYH11-5 Concluded

EYH11-6 Moon's Dry Cleaners

a–c.

EYH11-6 Concluded

Name _____

CAI11-1 General Motors

a.

_____
_____
_____
_____
_____
_____
_____
_____
_____
_____
_____
_____
_____
_____
_____
_____
_____
_____
_____
_____
_____
_____
_____
_____
_____
_____
_____
_____
_____
_____
_____

CAI11-1 General Motors

CAI11-1   Concluded

b.

P12-A1 Vancouver Equipment

a.

JOURNAL

PAGE _____

	DATE		DESCRIPTION	POST REF.	DEBIT	CREDIT	
1							1
2							2
3							3
4							4
5							5
6							6
7							7
8							8
9							9
10							10
11							11
12							12
13							13
14							14
15							15
16							16
17							17
18							18
19							19
20							20
21							21
22							22
23							23
24							24
25							25
26							26
27							27
28							28
29							29
30							30
31							31
32							32

P12-A1 Concluded

b.

P12-A2 Beltway Repro

a.

<table>
<tr><td align="center">JOURNAL</td><td></td><td></td><td align="center">PAGE</td><td></td></tr>
</table>

	DATE		DESCRIPTION	POST REF.	DEBIT	CREDIT	
1							1
2							2
3							3
4							4
5							5
6							6
7							7
8							8
9							9
10							10
11							11
12							12
13							13
14							14
15							15
16							16
17							17
18							18
19							19
20							20
21							21
22							22
23							23
24							24
25							25
26							26
27							27
28							28
29							29
30							30
31							31
32							32

P12-A2 Concluded

b.

JOURNAL

PAGE

	DATE		DESCRIPTION	POST REF.	DEBIT	CREDIT	
1							1
2							2
3							3
4							4
5							5
6							6
7							7
8							8
9							9
10							10
11							11
12							12
13							13
14							14
15							15
16							16
17							17
18							18
19							19
20							20
21							21
22							22
23							23
24							24
25							25
26							26
27							27
28							28
29							29
30							30
31							31
32							32

P12-A3 Ocean Enterprises, Inc.

a–b.

P12-A3 Concluded

P12-A4 Lockeford Lumber

a–c.

_____

_____

_____

_____

_____

_____

_____

_____

_____

_____

_____

_____

_____

_____

_____

_____

_____

_____

_____

_____

_____

_____

_____

_____

_____

_____

_____

_____

_____

_____

P12-A4 Concluded

P12-A5 Broadway Company

a.

Intangible Asset	Date Acquired	Cost	Life (Years)	Amortization (Cost/Life)
		$		$

b. _____
_____
_____
_____
_____
_____
_____
_____
_____
_____
_____
_____
_____
_____
_____
_____
_____
_____
_____
_____

P12-A5 Concluded

c.

JOURNAL

PAGE

	DATE		DESCRIPTION	POST REF.	DEBIT	CREDIT	
1							1
2							2
3							3
4							4
5							5
6							6
7							7
8							8
9							9
10							10
11							11
12							12
13							13
14							14
15							15
16							16
17							17
18							18
19							19
20							20
21							21
22							22
23							23
24							24
25							25
26							26
27							27
28							28
29							29
30							30
31							31
32							32

P12-B1 Hollywood Company

a.

JOURNAL

PAGE _____

	DATE		DESCRIPTION	POST REF.	DEBIT	CREDIT	
1							1
2							2
3							3
4							4
5							5
6							6
7							7
8							8
9							9
10							10
11							11
12							12
13							13
14							14
15							15
16							16
17							17
18							18
19							19
20							20
21							21
22							22
23							23
24							24
25							25
26							26
27							27
28							28
29							29
30							30
31							31
32							32

P12-B1 Concluded

b.

P12-B2 Lansing Regional Transit

a.

JOURNAL

PAGE ____

	DATE		DESCRIPTION	POST REF.	DEBIT	CREDIT	
1							1
2							2
3							3
4							4
5							5
6							6
7							7
8							8
9							9
10							10
11							11
12							12
13							13
14							14
15							15
16							16
17							17
18							18
19							19
20							20
21							21
22							22
23							23
24							24
25							25
26							26
27							27
28							28
29							29
30							30
31							31
32							32

P12-B2 Concluded

b.

JOURNAL

PAGE

	DATE		DESCRIPTION	POST REF.	DEBIT	CREDIT	
1							1
2							2
3							3
4							4
5							5
6							6
7							7
8							8
9							9
10							10
11							11
12							12
13							13
14							14
15							15
16							16
17							17
18							18
19							19
20							20
21							21
22							22
23							23
24							24
25							25
26							26
27							27
28							28
29							29
30							30
31							31
32							32

P12-B3 Third Avenue Mfg.

a–b.

P12-B3 Concluded

P12-B4 Bach Mining Company

a.

P12-B4   Concluded

b.

P12-B5 Golden State Company

a.

Intangible Asset	Cost	Life (Years)	Amortization (Cost/Life)
	$		$

b.

JOURNAL

PAGE _____

	DATE		DESCRIPTION	POST REF.	DEBIT	CREDIT	
1							1
2							2
3							3
4							4
5							5
6							6
7							7
8							8
9							9
10							10
11							11
12							12
13							13
14							14
15							15
16							16
17							17

P12-B5 Concluded

c.

EYH12-1 Asset Impairment

EYH12-1 Concluded

EYH12-2 Franchising in the U. S.

EYH12-2 Concluded

EYH12-3 Brand Value

a–b.

EYH12-3 Concluded

EYH12-4 Duracell International/Campbell Soup

a–d.

EYH12-4   Concluded

Name _____

EYH12-5

a–d.

EYH12-5 Concluded

EYH12-6 Dudley Finfrock

a–b.

EYH12-6 Concluded

Name _____

CAI12-1 Bristol-Myers Squibb

CAI12-1 Concluded

CAI12-1 Concluded

Comprehensive Problem 2 Wyatt Company

a.

Comprehensive Problem 2 Continued

b.

Wyatt Company

Balance Sheet

December 31, 19X8

Name _____

Comprehensive Problem 2 Continued

b.

Comprehensive Problem 2 Concluded

c.

Name _____

P13-A1 Quality Products

Quality Products

Balance Sheet

December 31, 19X2

P13-A1 Concluded

P13-A2 Long Island Company

a.

JOURNAL   PAGE

	DATE	DESCRIPTION	POST REF.	DEBIT	CREDIT	
1						1
2						2
3						3
4						4
5						5
6						6
7						7
8						8
9						9
10						10
11						11
12						12
13						13
14						14
15						15
16						16
17						17
18						18
19						19
20						20
21						21
22						22
23						23
24						24
25						25
26						26
27						27
28						28
29						29
30						30
31						31
32						32

P13-A2 Concluded

b.

JOURNAL

DATE	DESCRIPTION	POST REF.	DEBIT	CREDIT	
1					1
2					2
3					3
4					4
5					5
6					6
7					7
8					8
9					9
10					10
11					11
12					12
13					13
14					14

c.

Long Island Company

Balance Sheet

March 31, 19XX

P13-A3 D'Angelo Company

a. _____

_____

_____

_____

_____

_____

_____

_____

_____

_____

_____

JOURNAL   PAGE _____

	DATE		DESCRIPTION	POST REF.	DEBIT	CREDIT	
1							1
2							2
3							3
4							4
5							5
6							6
7							7
8							8
9							9
10							10
11							11
12							12
13							13
14							14
15							15
16							16
17							17
18							18
19							19
20							20

P13-A3 Concluded

b.

JOURNAL

PAGE _____

	DATE		DESCRIPTION	POST REF.	DEBIT	CREDIT	
1							1
2							2
3							3
4							4
5							5
6							6
7							7
8							8
9							9
10							10
11							11
12							12
13							13
14							14
15							15
16							16
17							17
18							18
19							19
20							20

P13-A4 LJP Company

a.

JOURNAL

PAGE

	DATE		DESCRIPTION	POST REF.	DEBIT	CREDIT	
1							1
2							2
3							3
4							4
5							5
6							6
7							7
8							8
9							9
10							10
11							11
12							12
13							13
14							14
15							15
16							16
17							17
18							18
19							19
20							20
21							21
22							22
23							23
24							24
25							25
26							26
27							27
28							28
29							29
30							30
31							31
32							32

P13-A4 Concluded

b.

JOURNAL

	DATE		DESCRIPTION	POST REF.	DEBIT	CREDIT	
1							1
2							2
3							3
4							4
5							5
6							6
7							7
8							8
9							9
10							10
11							11
12							12
13							13
14							14
15							15
16							16
17							17
18							18
19							19
20							20

c.

P13-A5 Starglo Cosmetics

a–b.

JOURNAL

	DATE		DESCRIPTION	POST REF.	DEBIT	CREDIT	
1							1
2							2
3							3
4							4
5							5
6							6
7							7
8							8
9							9
10							10
11							11
12							12
13							13
14							14
15							15
16							16
17							17
18							18
19							19
20							20
21							21
22							22
23							23
24							24
25							25
26							26
27							27
28							28
29							29
30							30
31							31
32							32

P13-A5 Concluded

c–d.

P13-B1 Advantage Company

Advantage Company

Balance Sheet

December 31, 19X7

P13-B1 Concluded

P13-B2 Visconti's

a.

JOURNAL

PAGE

	DATE		DESCRIPTION	POST REF.	DEBIT	CREDIT	
1							1
2							2
3							3
4							4
5							5
6							6
7							7
8							8
9							9
10							10
11							11
12							12
13							13
14							14
15							15
16							16
17							17
18							18
19							19
20							20
21							21
22							22
23							23
24							24
25							25
26							26
27							27
28							28
29							29
30							30
31							31
32							32

P13-B2 Concluded

b.

JOURNAL

	DATE		DESCRIPTION	POST REF.	DEBIT	CREDIT	
1							1
2							2
3							3
4							4
5							5
6							6
7							7
8							8
9							9
10							10
11							11
12							12
13							13
14							14

c.

Visconti's

Balance Sheet

December 31, 19XX

Name _____

P13-B3 Chung, Inc.

a.

	DATE		DESCRIPTION	POST REF.	DEBIT	CREDIT	
1							1
2							2
3							3
4							4
5							5
6							6
7							7
8							8
9							9
10							10
11							11
12							12
13							13
14							14
15							15
16							16
17							17
18							18
19							19
20							20
21							21
22							22
23							23
24							24
25							25
26							26
27							27
28							28
29							29
30							30
31							31
32							32

JOURNAL PAGE

P13-B3 Concluded

b–c.

JOURNAL   PAGE

	DATE		DESCRIPTION	POST REF.	DEBIT	CREDIT	
1							1
2							2
3							3
4							4
5							5
6							6
7							7
8							8
9							9
10							10
11							11
12							12
13							13
14							14
15							15
16							16
17							17
18							18
19							19

c.

Chung, Inc.

Balance Sheet

June 30, 19XX

P13-B4 Knight Wholesale

a.

JOURNAL

PAGE _____

	DATE		DESCRIPTION	POST REF.	DEBIT	CREDIT	
1							1
2							2
3							3
4							4
5							5
6							6
7							7
8							8
9							9
10							10
11							11
12							12
13							13
14							14
15							15
16							16
17							17
18							18
19							19
20							20
21							21
22							22
23							23
24							24
25							25
26							26
27							27
28							28
29							29
30							30
31							31
32							32

P13-B4 Concluded

b.

JOURNAL

PAGE

	DATE		DESCRIPTION	POST REF.	DEBIT	CREDIT	
1							1
2							2
3							3
4							4
5							5
6							6
7							7
8							8
9							9
10							10
11							11
12							12
13							13
14							14
15							15
16							16
17							17
18							18
19							19

c.

P13-B5 Deluxe Ceramics

a–b.

	JOURNAL				PAGE	

	DATE		DESCRIPTION	POST REF.	DEBIT	CREDIT	
1							1
2							2
3							3
4							4
5							5
6							6
7							7
8							8
9							9
10							10
11							11
12							12
13							13
14							14
15							15
16							16
17							17
18							18
19							19
20							20
21							21
22							22
23							23
24							24
25							25
26							26
27							27
28							28
29							29
30							30
31							31
32							32

P13-B5 Concluded

c–d.

EYH13-1 Contingency Disclosures

EYH13-1   Concluded

EYH13-2 Postretirement Benefits

a.

EYH13-2 Concluded

b.

EYH13-3 Fringe Benefit Costs

EYH13-3 Concluded

Name _____

EYH13-4 Sprint/H. J. Heinz

a–c.

EYH13-4 Concluded

EYH13-4 Concluded

EYH13-5

a–c.

EYH13-5 Concluded

EYH13-6 City of Lawndale

a–c.

EYH13-6 Concluded

Name _____

CAI13-1 The Boeing Company

CAI13-1 Concluded

P14-A1 Atlanta Sound & TV

a–f.

P14-A1 Concluded

P14-A2 Ballpark Industries

a.

Ballpark Industries

Schedule

	NET INCOME	ASSETS	LIABILITIES	OWNER'S EQUITY

P14-A2 Concluded

b.

P14-A3 I Love Yogurt

I Love Yogurt

Schedule of Profit Earned

19X2

P14-A3 Concluded

Name _____

P14-A4 Bennett Developers

a.

_____
_____
_____
_____
_____
_____
_____
_____

b.

Bennett Developers

Schedule

	YEAR	ACTUAL COSTS INCURRED	PERCENTAGE OF WORK COMPLETED	PROFIT RECOGNIZED	

P14-A4 Concluded

c.

Bennett Developers

Schedule

	YEAR	CASH COLLECTED	PROFIT PERCENTAGE	PROFIT RECOGNIZED	

P14-A5 Key Manufacturing

a–c.

JOURNAL   PAGE ____

	DATE		DESCRIPTION	POST REF.	DEBIT	CREDIT	
1							1
2							2
3							3
4							4
5							5
6							6
7							7
8							8
9							9
10							10
11							11
12							12
13							13
14							14
15							15
16							16
17							17
18							18
19							19
20							20
21							21
22							22
23							23
24							24
25							25
26							26
27							27
28							28
29							29
30							30
31							31
32							32

P14-A5   Concluded

JOURNAL

	DATE		DESCRIPTION	POST REF.	DEBIT	CREDIT	
1							1
2							2
3							3
4							4
5							5
6							6
7							7
8							8
9							9
10							10
11							11
12							12
13							13
14							14
15							15
16							16
17							17
18							18
19							19
20							20
21							21
22							22
23							23
24							24
25							25
26							26
27							27
28							28
29							29
30							30
31							31
32							32

P14-B1 Westside Tool & Die, Inc.

a–f.

P14-B1 Concluded

P14-B2 Reno Enterprises

a.

Reno Enterprises

Schedule

	NET INCOME (LOSS)	ASSETS	LIABILITIES	OWNER'S EQUITY

P14-B2 Concluded

b.

P14-B3 Dr. Allison Hardy

P14-B3 Concluded

P14-B4 San Diego Shipyards

a.

San Diego Shipyards

Schedule

	YEAR	ACTUAL COSTS INCURRED	PERCENTAGE OF WORK COMPLETED	PROFIT RECOGNIZED	

P14-B4 Concluded

b.

San Diego Shipyards

Schedule

	YEAR	CASH COLLECTED	PROFIT PERCENTAGE	PROFIT RECOGNIZED

P14-B5 Topaz Enterprises

a.

JOURNAL

PAGE _____

	DATE	DESCRIPTION	POST REF.	DEBIT	CREDIT	
1						1
2						2
3						3
4						4
5						5
6						6
7						7
8						8
9						9
10						10
11						11
12						12
13						13
14						14
15						15
16						16
17						17
18						18
19						19
20						20
21						21
22						22
23						23
24						24
25						25
26						26
27						27
28						28
29						29
30						30
31						31
32						32

P14-B5 Concluded

b.

JOURNAL

	DATE		DESCRIPTION	POST REF.	DEBIT	CREDIT	
1							1
2							2
3							3
4							4
5							5
6							6
7							7
8							8
9							9
10							10
11							11
12							12
13							13
14							14
15							15
16							16
17							17
18							18
19							19
20							20
21							21
22							22
23							23
24							24
25							25
26							26
27							27
28							28
29							29
30							30
31							31
32							32

EYH14-1 Controversial Standards

EYH14-1 Concluded

EYH14-2 FASB Statement Review

a–e.

EYH14-2 Concluded

EYH14-3 Revenue Recognition

EYH14-3 Concluded

EYH14-4 Reebok International

a–d.

EYH14-4 Concluded

EYH14-4 Concluded

EYH14-5

a–d.

EYH14-5 Concluded

EYH14-6 Arens Real Estate

a–e.

EYH14-6 Concluded

Name _____

CAI14-1 Black & Decker

CAI14-1 Concluded

P15-A1 Guinn, Horton, & Randall

a.

JOURNAL   PAGE

	DATE	DESCRIPTION	POST REF.	DEBIT	CREDIT	
1						1
2						2
3						3
4						4
5						5
6						6
7						7
8						8
9						9
10						10
11						11
12						12
13						13
14						14
15						15
16						16
17						17
18						18
19						19
20						20
21						21
22						22
23						23
24						24
25						25
26						26
27						27
28						28
29						29
30						30
31						31
32						32

P15-A1 Concluded

b.

Guinn, Horton, & Randall

Statement of Partners' Equity

For the Year Ended December 31, 19X4

	QUINN	HORTON	RANDALL	TOTAL

c.

Guinn, Horton, & Randall

Balance Sheet

December 31, 19X4

Name _____

P15-A2 Webster, Mullins, & Hardaway

a.

Net Income (Loss)	Webster	Mullins	Hardaway
$80,000			
10,000			
(20,000)			

Supporting Calculations:

P15-A2 Concluded

b.

JOURNAL

PAGE

	DATE	DESCRIPTION	POST REF.	DEBIT	CREDIT	
1						1
2						2
3						3
4						4
5						5
6						6
7						7
8						8
9						9
10						10
11						11
12						12
13						13
14						14
15						15

c.

Webster, Mullins, & Hardaway

Balance Sheet

December 31, 19X6

P15-A3 Mantle, Maris, & Berra

a.

JOURNAL   PAGE

	DATE	DESCRIPTION	POST REF.	DEBIT	CREDIT	
1						1
2						2
3						3
4						4
5						5
6						6
7						7
8						8
9						9
10						10
11						11
12						12
13						13
14						14
15						15
16						16
17						17
18						18
19						19
20						20
21						21
22						22
23						23
24						24
25						25
26						26
27						27
28						28
29						29
30						30
31						31
32						32

P15-A3 Concluded

JOURNAL

	DATE	DESCRIPTION	POST REF.	DEBIT	CREDIT	
1						1
2						2
3						3
4						4
5						5
6						6
7						7
8						8
9						9
10						10
11						11
12						12
13						13
14						14
15						15
16						16
17						17
18						18
19						19
20						20

b.

P15-A4 Pulaski, Smith, & Freeman

a.

b.

JOURNAL   PAGE

	DATE	DESCRIPTION	POST REF.	DEBIT	CREDIT	
1						1
2						2
3						3
4						4
5						5
6						6
7						7
8						8
9						9
10						10
11						11
12						12
13						13
14						14

P15-A4 Concluded

c–d.

P15-A5 Manny, Moe, & Abe

a.

JOURNAL   PAGE

	DATE		DESCRIPTION	POST REF.	DEBIT	CREDIT	
1							1
2							2
3							3
4							4
5							5
6							6
7							7
8							8
9							9
10							10
11							11
12							12
13							13
14							14
15							15
16							16
17							17
18							18
19							19
20							20
21							21
22							22
23							23
24							24
25							25
26							26
27							27
28							28
29							29
30							30
31							31
32							32

P15-A5 Concluded

b.

JOURNAL

PAGE

	DATE		DESCRIPTION	POST REF.	DEBIT	CREDIT	
1							1
2							2
3							3
4							4
5							5
6							6
7							7
8							8
9							9
10							10
11							11
12							12
13							13
14							14
15							15
16							16
17							17
18							18
19							19
20							20
21							21
22							22
23							23
24							24
25							25
26							26
27							27

P15-B1 Parker, Bowen, & Norton

a.

JOURNAL   PAGE

	DATE		DESCRIPTION	POST REF.	DEBIT	CREDIT	
1							1
2							2
3							3
4							4
5							5
6							6
7							7
8							8
9							9
10							10
11							11
12							12
13							13
14							14
15							15
16							16
17							17
18							18
19							19
20							20
21							21
22							22
23							23
24							24
25							25
26							26
27							27
28							28
29							29
30							30
31							31
32							32

P15-B1 Concluded

b.

Parker, Bowen, & Norton

Statement of Partners' Equity

For the Year Ended December 31, 19XX

	PARKER	BOWEN	NORTON	TOTAL

c.

P15-B2 Jackson, Hudson, & Rice

a.

Jackson, Hudson, & Rice
Division of Net Income

	JACKSON	HUDSON	RICE	TOTAL

P15-B2 Concluded

b.

JOURNAL

PAGE

	DATE		DESCRIPTION	POST REF.	DEBIT	CREDIT	
1							1
2							2
3							3
4							4
5							5
6							6
7							7
8							8
9							9
10							10
11							11
12							12
13							13
14							14
15							15
16							16
17							17

c.

Jackson, Hudson, and Rice

Balance Sheet

December 31, 19X2

P15-B3 Barden, Larkins, & Winter

a.

JOURNAL   PAGE _____

	DATE	DESCRIPTION	POST REF.	DEBIT	CREDIT	
1						1
2						2
3						3
4						4
5						5
6						6
7						7
8						8
9						9
10						10
11						11
12						12
13						13
14						14
15						15
16						16
17						17
18						18
19						19
20						20
21						21
22						22
23						23
24						24
25						25
26						26
27						27
28						28
29						29
30						30
31						31
32						32

P15-B3 Concluded

	DATE		DESCRIPTION	POST REF.	DEBIT	CREDIT	
1							1
2							2
3							3
4							4
5							5
6							6
7							7
8							8
9							9
10							10
11							11
12							12
13							13
14							14
15							15
16							16
17							17
18							18
19							19
20							20

JOURNAL   PAGE

b.

P15-B4 Hecht, Livingston, & Martin

a–b.

(blank ruled lines)

c.

JOURNAL   PAGE

	DATE		DESCRIPTION	POST REF.	DEBIT	CREDIT	
1							1
2							2
3							3
4							4
5							5
6							6
7							7
8							8
9							9
10							10
11							11
12							12
13							13
14							14

P15-B4 Concluded

d–e.

P15-B5 Unser, Jenkins, & Paulus

a.

JOURNAL   PAGE

	DATE		DESCRIPTION	POST REF.	DEBIT	CREDIT	
1							1
2							2
3							3
4							4
5							5
6							6
7							7
8							8
9							9
10							10
11							11
12							12
13							13
14							14
15							15
16							16
17							17
18							18
19							19
20							20
21							21
22							22
23							23
24							24
25							25
26							26
27							27
28							28
29							29
30							30
31							31
32							32

P15-B5 Continued

b.

JOURNAL

	DATE		DESCRIPTION	POST REF.	DEBIT	CREDIT	
1							1
2							2
3							3
4							4
5							5
6							6
7							7
8							8
9							9
10							10
11							11
12							12
13							13
14							14
15							15
16							16
17							17
18							18
19							19
20							20
21							21
22							22
23							23
24							24
25							25
26							26
27							27
28							28
29							29
30							30
31							31
32							32

P15-B5 Continued

c.

	DATE		DESCRIPTION	POST REF.	DEBIT	CREDIT	
1							1
2							2
3							3
4							4
5							5
6							6
7							7
8							8
9							9
10							10
11							11
12							12
13							13
14							14
15							15
16							16
17							17
18							18
19							19
20							20
21							21
22							22
23							23
24							24
25							25
26							26
27							27
28							28
29							29
30							30
31							31
32							32

JOURNAL   PAGE

P15-B5 Concluded

JOURNAL

PAGE

	DATE		DESCRIPTION	POST REF.	DEBIT	CREDIT	
1							1
2							2
3							3
4							4
5							5
6							6
7							7
8							8
9							9
10							10
11							11
12							12
13							13
14							14
15							15
16							16
17							17
18							18
19							19
20							20
21							21
22							22
23							23
24							24
25							25
26							26
27							27
28							28
29							29
30							30
31							31
32							32

EYH15-1 Family Partnerships

EYH15-1   Concluded

EYH15-2   Partnership Agreements

EYH15-2 Concluded

EYH15-3 Limited Liability Partnerships

EYH15-3 Concluded

EYH15-4 Knapp, Shingler, & Smith

a–e.

EYH15-4 Concluded

CAI15-1 Harrison, O'Brien, & Weinstein

CAI15-1 Concluded

P16-A1 Furlow Industries

a–c.

P16-A1 Concluded

Name _____

P16-A2 Porter Furniture

a.

JOURNAL   PAGE _____

	DATE		DESCRIPTION	POST REF.	DEBIT	CREDIT	
1							1
2							2
3							3
4							4
5							5
6							6
7							7
8							8
9							9
10							10
11							11
12							12
13							13
14							14
15							15
16							16
17							17
18							18
19							19
20							20
21							21
22							22
23							23
24							24
25							25
26							26
27							27
28							28
29							29
30							30
31							31
32							32

P16-A2 Concluded

b.

Porter Furniture

Stockholders' Equity Section—Balance Sheet

December 31, 19XX

c.

P16-A3 Rocky Mountain, Inc.

Rocky Mountain, Inc.

Stockholders' Equity Section—Balance Sheet

December 31, 19X6

P16-A3 Concluded

P16-A4 Hastings Corporation

1–6.

P16-A4 Concluded

P16-A5 Stop and Save, Inc.

a–c.

P16-A5 Concluded

P16-B1 Hendricks Corporation

a–c.

P16-B1 Concluded

_____

_____

_____

_____

_____

_____

_____

_____

_____

_____

_____

_____

_____

_____

_____

_____

_____

_____

_____

_____

_____

_____

_____

_____

_____

_____

_____

_____

_____

_____

_____

P16-B2 Ventures, Inc.

a.

JOURNAL

PAGE

DATE		DESCRIPTION	POST REF.	DEBIT	CREDIT	
1						1
2						2
3						3
4						4
5						5
6						6
7						7
8						8
9						9
10						10
11						11
12						12
13						13
14						14
15						15
16						16
17						17
18						18
19						19
20						20
21						21
22						22
23						23
24						24
25						25
26						26
27						27
28						28
29						29
30						30
31						31
32						32

P16-B2 Concluded

b.

Ventures, Inc.

Stockholders' Equity Section—Balance Sheet

March 31, 19XX

c.

P16-B3 Treasure City

Treasure City

Stockholders' Equity Section—Balance Sheet

December 31, 19XX

P16-B3   Concluded

P16-B4 Graceland Corporation

a–g.

P16-B4 Concluded

Name _____

Chapter 16   649

P16-B5 Travel Resorts, Inc.

a–c.

_____

_____

_____

_____

_____

_____

_____

_____

_____

_____

_____

_____

_____

_____

_____

_____

_____

_____

_____

_____

_____

_____

_____

_____

_____

_____

_____

_____

_____

_____

_____

_____

_____

_____

_____

P16-B5 Concluded

EYH16-1   Organizing a Corporation

a.

EYH16-1   Concluded

b.

EYH16-2 Stock Price Movements

EYH16-2 Concluded

EYH16-3 Initial Public Offerings

EYH16-3 Concluded

EYH16-4 MCI/Capital Cities

a–c.

EYH16-4 Concluded

EYH16-5

a–c.

EYH16-5 Concluded

EYH16-6 Sweat Equity

a–c.

EYH16-6 Concluded

CAI16-1 American Brands, Inc.

CAI16-1 Concluded

P17-A1 You Fix It, Inc.

a.

JOURNAL

PAGE _____

	DATE		DESCRIPTION	POST REF.	DEBIT	CREDIT	
1							1
2							2
3							3
4							4
5							5
6							6
7							7
8							8
9							9
10							10
11							11
12							12
13							13
14							14
15							15
16							16
17							17
18							18
19							19
20							20
21							21
22							22
23							23
24							24
25							25
26							26
27							27
28							28
29							29
30							30
31							31
32							32

P17-A1 Concluded

JOURNAL

PAGE

DATE		DESCRIPTION	POST REF.	DEBIT	CREDIT	
1						1
2						2
3						3
4						4
5						5
6						6
7						7
8						8
9						9
10						10
11						11
12						12
13						13
14						14

b.

You Fix It, Inc.

Stockholders' Equity Section—Balance Sheet

December 31, 19X8

P17-A2 Goodrich Metals

a.

		JOURNAL			PAGE	

	DATE		DESCRIPTION	POST REF.	DEBIT	CREDIT	
1							1
2							2
3							3
4							4
5							5
6							6
7							7
8							8
9							9
10							10
11							11
12							12
13							13
14							14
15							15
16							16
17							17
18							18
19							19
20							20
21							21
22							22
23							23
24							24
25							25
26							26
27							27
28							28
29							29
30							30
31							31
32							32

P17-A2 Concluded

JOURNAL

PAGE

	DATE	DESCRIPTION	POST REF.	DEBIT	CREDIT	
1						1
2						2
3						3
4						4
5						5
6						6
7						7
8						8
9						9
10						10
11						11

b.

Goodrich Metals

Stockholders' Equity Section—Balance Sheet

December 31, 19XX

P17-A3 Roadside Equipment

a.

Roadside Equipment

Statement of Retained Earnings

For the Year Ended December 31, 19X2

P17-A3 Concluded

b.

Roadside Equipment

Stockholders' Equity Section—Balance Sheet

December 31, 19X2

P17-A4   Brady Corporation

a.

P17-A4   Concluded

b.

	Brady Corporation									
	Income Statement									
	For the Year Ended December 31, 19X4									

P17-A5 Astro, Inc.

Astro, Inc.

Income Statement

For the Year Ended November 30, 19X3

P17-A5 Concluded

P17-B1 Bridge Corporation

a.

Date	Common Stock	Paid-in Capital in Excess of Par	Retained Earnings	Treasury Stock
Jan. 15				
Feb. 15				

P17-B1   Concluded

b.

Bridge Corporation

Stockholders' Equity Section—Balance Sheet

December 31, 19X6

P17-B2 Home Cooking, Inc.

a.

<h1 style="text-align:center">JOURNAL</h1>   PAGE

	DATE		DESCRIPTION	POST REF.	DEBIT	CREDIT	
1							1
2							2
3							3
4							4
5							5
6							6
7							7
8							8
9							9
10							10
11							11
12							12
13							13
14							14
15							15
16							16
17							17
18							18
19							19
20							20
21							21
22							22
23							23
24							24
25							25
26							26
27							27
28							28
29							29
30							30
31							31
32							32

P17-B2 Concluded

JOURNAL

	DATE	DESCRIPTION	POST REF.	DEBIT	CREDIT	
1						1
2						2
3						3
4						4
5						5
6						6
7						7
8						8
9						9
10						10
11						11

b.

Home Cooking, Inc.

Stockholders' Equity Section—Balance Sheet

December 31, 19XX

P17-B3 Mansfield Merchants, Inc.

a.

Mansfield Merchants, Inc.

Statement of Retained Earnings

For the Year Ended December 31, 19X9

P17-B3 Concluded

Mansfield Merchants, Inc.

Stockholders' Equity Section—Balance Sheet

December 31, 19X9

P17-B4   Champion, Inc.

a.

P17-B4 Concluded

b.

Champion, Inc.

Income Statement

For the Year Ended December 31, 19XX

P17-B5 Far West Importers, Inc.

Far West Importers, Inc.

Income Statement

For the Year Ended December 31, 19X5

P17-B5 Concluded

EYH17-1 Stock Dividends/Splits

EYH17-1   Concluded

EYH17-2 Reporting Tone

EYH17-2 Concluded

EYH17-3 Earnings Information

EYH17-3 Concluded

EYH17-4 Clorox/The Home Depot

a–d.

EYH17-4 Concluded

EYH17-5

a–d.

EYH17-5 Concluded

EYH17-6 Wilderness Herbal Teas

EYH17-6 Concluded

CAI17-1   H & R Block, Inc.

CAI17-1 Concluded

P18-A1 Richmond Corporation

a–e.

P18-A1 Concluded

P18-A2 Alliance Stores

	Case A	Case B	Case C
a. Cash inflow on the issuance date	_____	_____	_____
b. Total cash outflow through maturity	_____	_____	_____
c. Total borrowing cost over the life of the bond issue	_____	_____	_____
d. Interest expense for the year ended December 31, 19X1	_____	_____	_____
e. Amortization for the year ended December 31, 19X1	_____	_____	_____
f. Unamortized premium as of December 31, 19X1	_____	_____	_____
g. Unamortized discount as of December 31, 19X1	_____	_____	_____
h. Bond carrying value as of December 31, 19X1	_____	_____	_____

Supporting calculations: _____

_____

_____

_____

_____

_____

_____

_____

_____

_____

_____

_____

_____

_____

_____

_____

_____

_____

P18-A2 Concluded

P18-A3 Hickory Products

a.

JOURNAL

PAGE

	DATE	DESCRIPTION	POST REF.	DEBIT	CREDIT	
1						1
2						2
3						3
4						4
5						5
6						6
7						7
8						8
9						9
10						10
11						11
12						12
13						13
14						14
15						15
16						16
17						17
18						18
19						19
20						20
21						21
22						22
23						23
24						24
25						25
26						26
27						27
28						28
29						29
30						30
31						31
32						32

P18-A3 Concluded

b–c.

_____
_____
_____
_____
_____
_____
_____
_____
_____
_____
_____
_____
_____
_____
_____
_____
_____
_____
_____
_____

d.

JOURNAL   PAGE

	DATE	DESCRIPTION	POST REF.	DEBIT	CREDIT	
1						1
2						2
3						3
4						4
5						5
6						6
7						7
8						8
9						9
10						10
11						11

P18-A4 Burk Corporation

a–c.

P18-A4 Concluded

d–e.

JOURNAL

PAGE

	DATE	DESCRIPTION	POST REF.	DEBIT	CREDIT	
1						1
2						2
3						3
4						4
5						5
6						6
7						7
8						8
9						9
10						10
11						11
12						12
13						13
14						14
15						15
16						16
17						17
18						18
19						19
20						20
21						21
22						22
23						23
24						24
25						25
26						26
27						27
28						28
29						29
30						30
31						31
32						32

P18-A5 Bombay Imports

a.

JOURNAL

DATE	DESCRIPTION	POST REF.	DEBIT	CREDIT
1				
2				
3				
4				
5				
6				
7				
8				
9				
10				
11				
12				
13				
14				
15				

b.

DISCOUNT AMORTIZATION SCHEDULE

Semi-Annual Interest Period	Effective Semi-Annual Interest Expense	Semi-Annual Interest Payments	Discount Amortization	Bond Discount Balance	End-of-Period Bond Carrying Value
Issue date				_____	_____
_____	_____	_____	_____	_____	_____
_____	_____	_____	_____	_____	_____
_____	_____	_____	_____	_____	_____
_____	_____	_____	_____	_____	_____
_____	_____	_____	_____	_____	_____
_____	_____	_____	_____	_____	_____

P18-A5 Concluded

b.

JOURNAL   PAGE

	DATE		DESCRIPTION	POST REF.	DEBIT	CREDIT	
1							1
2							2
3							3
4							4
5							5
6							6
7							7
8							8
9							9
10							10
11							11
12							12
13							13
14							14
15							15

c.

Bombay Imports

Balance Sheet

December 31, 19X7

P18-A6 Regal Ice Cream

a.

_____
_____
_____
_____
_____
_____
_____
_____
_____
_____

b.

JOURNAL   PAGE _____

	DATE	DESCRIPTION	POST REF.	DEBIT	CREDIT	
1						1
2						2
3						3
4						4
5						5
6						6
7						7
8						8
9						9
10						10
11						11
12						12
13						13
14						14
15						15
16						16
17						17
18						18
19						19
20						20
21						21

P18-A6 Concluded

c.

JOURNAL

	DATE	DESCRIPTION	POST REF.	DEBIT	CREDIT	
1						1
2						2
3						3
4						4
5						5
6						6
7						7
8						8
9						9
10						10
11						11
12						12
13						13
14						14
15						15
16						16
17						17

d.

Regal Ice Cream

Balance Sheet

December 31, 19X2

P18-B1 American Media, Inc.

a–d.

P18-B1 Concluded

P18-B2 Broadway Corporation

a.

Case 1

1. Proceeds from bond issuance
2. Total cash outflow through maturity
3. Total borrowing cost over the life of the bond issue
4. Amortization for 19X5
5. Interest expense for 19X5
6. Unamortized premium or discount , if any, on December 31, 19X5
7. Bond carrying value on December 31, 19X5

b.

Case 2

1. Proceeds from bond issuance
2. Total cash outflow through maturity
3. Total borrowing cost over the life of the bond issue
4. Amortization for 19X5
5. Interest expense for 19X5
6. Unamortized premium or discount , if any, on December 31, 19X5
7. Bond carrying value on December 31, 19X5

c.

Case 3

1. Proceeds from bond issuance
2. Total cash outflow through maturity
3. Total borrowing cost over the life of the bond issue
4. Amortization for 19X5
5. Interest expense for 19X5
6. Unamortized premium or discount , if any, on December 31, 19X5
7. Bond carrying value on December 31, 19X5

P17-B2 Concluded

a–c.

Supporting calculations:

P18-B3 Taylor Corporation

a.

JOURNAL   PAGE

	DATE		DESCRIPTION	POST REF.	DEBIT	CREDIT	
1							1
2							2
3							3
4							4
5							5
6							6
7							7
8							8
9							9
10							10
11							11
12							12
13							13
14							14
15							15
16							16
17							17
18							18
19							19
20							20
21							21
22							22
23							23
24							24
25							25
26							26
27							27

b. _____

_____

_____

_____

_____

P18-B3 Concluded

c.

Taylor Corporation

Balance Sheet

December 31, 19X1

d.

JOURNAL   PAGE

	DATE		DESCRIPTION	POST REF.	DEBIT	CREDIT	
1							1
2							2
3							3
4							4
5							5
6							6
7							7
8							8
9							9
10							10
11							11
12							12
13							13
14							14
15							15

P18-B4 Zeta Corporation

a–c.

P18-B4 Concluded

d–e.

JOURNAL   PAGE

	DATE		DESCRIPTION	POST REF.	DEBIT	CREDIT	
1							1
2							2
3							3
4							4
5							5
6							6
7							7
8							8
9							9
10							10
11							11
12							12
13							13
14							14
15							15
16							16
17							17
18							18
19							19
20							20
21							21
22							22
23							23
24							24
25							25
26							26
27							27
28							28
29							29
30							30
31							31
32							32

P18-B5 Hilo Electronics

a.

JOURNAL   PAGE

	DATE		DESCRIPTION	POST REF.	DEBIT	CREDIT	
1							1
2							2
3							3
4							4
5							5
6							6
7							7
8							8
9							9
10							10
11							11
12							12
13							13
14							14
15							15

b.

PREMIUM AMORTIZATION SCHEDULE

Semi-Annual Interest Period	Effective Semi-Annual Interest Expense	Semi-Annual Interest Payments	Premium Amortization	Bond Premium Balance	End-of-Period Bond Carrying Value
Issue Date				_____	_____
_____	_____	_____	_____	_____	_____
_____	_____	_____	_____	_____	_____
_____	_____	_____	_____	_____	_____
_____	_____	_____	_____	_____	_____
_____	_____	_____	_____	_____	_____
_____	_____	_____	_____	_____	_____
_____	_____	_____	_____	_____	_____
_____	_____	_____	_____	_____	_____

P18-B5 Concluded

b.

JOURNAL   PAGE

	DATE	DESCRIPTION	POST REF.	DEBIT	CREDIT	
1						1
2						2
3						3
4						4
5						5
6						6
7						7
8						8
9						9
10						10
11						11
12						12
13						13
14						14
15						15
16						16

c.

Hilo Electronics

Balance Sheet

December 31, 19X5

P18-B6 Oak Harbor Corporation

a. _____

_____

_____

_____

_____

_____

_____

_____

_____

b.

JOURNAL   PAGE _____

	DATE		DESCRIPTION	POST REF.	DEBIT	CREDIT	
1							1
2							2
3							3
4							4
5							5
6							6
7							7
8							8
9							9
10							10
11							11
12							12
13							13
14							14
15							15
16							16
17							17
18							18
19							19
20							20
21							21
22							22
23							23

P18-B6 Continued

c.

Oak Harbor Corporation

Balance Sheet

December 31, 19XX

d.

P18-B6 Continued

JOURNAL

	DATE		DESCRIPTION	POST REF.	DEBIT	CREDIT	
1							1
2							2
3							3
4							4
5							5
6							6
7							7
8							8
9							9
10							10
11							11
12							12
13							13
14							14
15							15
16							16
17							17
18							18
19							19
20							20
21							21
22							22
23							23
24							24
25							25
26							26
27							27
28							28
29							29
30							30
31							31
32							32

P18-B6 Concluded

Oak Harbor Corporation

Balance Sheet

December 31, 19XX

EYH18-1   Bond Ratings

_____
_____
_____
_____
_____
_____
_____
_____
_____
_____
_____
_____
_____
_____
_____
_____
_____
_____
_____
_____
_____
_____
_____
_____
_____
_____
_____
_____
_____
_____

EYH18-1   Bond Ratings

EYH18-1   Concluded

EYH18-2 Bond Financing

EYH18-2 Concluded

EYH18-3 Bond Investments

EYH18-3 Concluded

EYH18-4 Reebok International/Procter & Gamble

a–d.

EYH18-4 Concluded

Name _____

EYH18-5

a–d.

EYH18-5 Concluded

EYH18-6 Monet Fashion

a–d.

EYH18-6 Concluded

CAI18-1 AT&T

CAI18-1 Concluded

Comprehensive Problem 3 Houston Consulting

F&S Systems Design

Comprehensive Problem 3 Continued

Interstate Processing

JOURNAL

PAGE

	DATE		DESCRIPTION	POST REF.	DEBIT	CREDIT	
1							1
2							2
3							3
4							4
5							5
6							6
7							7
8							8
9							9
10							10
11							11
12							12
13							13
14							14
15							15
16							16
17							17
18							18
19							19
20							20
21							21
22							22
23							23
24							24
25							25
26							26
27							27
28							28
29							29
30							30
31							31
32							32

Comprehensive Problem 3 Continued

JOURNAL

PAGE _____

	DATE		DESCRIPTION	POST REF.	DEBIT	CREDIT	
1							1
2							2
3							3
4							4
5							5
6							6
7							7
8							8
9							9
10							10
11							11
12							12
13							13
14							14
15							15
16							16
17							17
18							18
19							19
20							20
21							21
22							22
23							23
24							24
25							25
26							26
27							27
28							28
29							29
30							30
31							31
32							32

Comprehensive Problem 3 Continued

Interstate Processing

Stockholders' Equity

Comprehensive Problem 3 Continued

Security Computers

Security Computers

Income Statement

For the Year Ended June 30, 19X8

Comprehensive Problem 3 Continued

Comprehensive Problem 3 Continued

CompuTech, Inc.

Comprehensive Problem 3 Concluded

Data Services

JOURNAL

PAGE

	DATE		DESCRIPTION	POST REF.	DEBIT	CREDIT	
1							1
2							2
3							3
4							4
5							5
6							6
7							7
8							8
9							9
10							10
11							11
12							12
13							13
14							14
15							15
16							16
17							17
18							18
19							19

Data Services

Balance Sheet

December 31, 19X8

P19-A1   Maui Corporation

a.

P19-A1 Concluded

b.

	Operating Activity	Investing Activity	Financing Activity	Noncash Investing/Financing Activity
1.				
2.				
3.				
4.				
5.				
6.				
7.				
8.				
9.				
10.				
11.				
12.				

P19-A2 Caruso's Peppers

a.

	Caruso's Peppers	
	Operating Activities Section—Statement of Cash Flows	
	Direct Method	

P19-A2 Concluded

b.

	Caruso's Peppers
	Operating Activities Section—Statement of Cash Flows
	Indirect Method

P19-A3 Hair Transplant Center

a.

Hair Transplant Center

Statement of Cash Flows

For the Quarter Ended March 31, 19X5

P19-A3 Concluded

b.

P19-A4 Sign Graphics, Inc.

a.

Sign Graphics, Inc.

Operating Activities Section—Statement of Cash Flows

Direct Method

Sign Graphics, Inc.

Operating Activities Section—Statement of Cash Flows

Indirect Method

P19-A4 Concluded

b.

Sign Graphics, Inc.

Investing Activities Section—Statement of Cash Flows

Sign Graphics, Inc.

Financing Activities Section—Statement of Cash Flows

P19-A5 Goodrich Company

a.

Goodrich Company

Statement of Cash Flows

For the Year Ended December 31, 19X2

P19-A5 Continued

P19-A6 Goodrich Company

a.

Goodrich Company

Work Sheet for Statement of Cash Flows

For the Year Ended December 31, 19X2

	ACCOUNT BALANCES 12/31/X1	ANALYSIS OF TRANSACTIONS—19X2		ACCOUNT BALANCES 12/31/X2	
		DEBIT	CREDIT		
1					1
2					2
3					3
4					4
5					5
6					6
7					7
8					8
9					9
10					10
11					11
12					12
13					13
14					14
15					15
16					16
17					17
18					18
19					19
20					20
21					21
22					22
23					23
24					24
25					25
26					26
27					27
28					28
29					29
30					30
31					31
32					32
33					33
34					34
35					35
36					36
37					37

P19-A6 Concluded

b.

Goodrich Company

Statement of Cash Flows

For the Year Ended December 31, 19X2

P19-B1 St. Thomas Corporation

a.

P19-B1 Concluded

	Operating Activity	Investing Activity	Financing Activity	Noncash Investing/Financing Activity
1.				
2.				
3.				
4.				
5.				
6.				
7.				
8.				
9.				
10.				
11.				
12.				

P19-B2 Fairfield General, Inc.

a.

Fairfield General, Inc.

Operating Activities Section—Statement of Cash Flows

Direct Method

P19-B2 Concluded

b.

	Fairfield General, Inc.

Operating Activities Section—Statement of Cash Flows

Indirect Method

P19-B3 Tulsa Bulldogs

a.

Tulsa Bulldogs
Statement of Cash Flows
For the Year Ended September 30, 19X2

P19-B3 Concluded

b.

P19-B4 Patel, Inc.

a.

Patel, Inc.

Operating Activities Section—Statement of Cash Flows

Direct Method

Patel, Inc.

Operating Activities Section—Statement of Cash Flows

Indirect Method

P19-B4 Concluded

b.

<table>
<tr><td colspan="2" align="center">Patel, Inc.</td></tr>
<tr><td colspan="2" align="center">Investing Activities Section—Statement of Cash Flows</td></tr>
</table>

<table>
<tr><td colspan="2" align="center">Patel, Inc.</td></tr>
<tr><td colspan="2" align="center">Financing Activities Section—Statement of Cash Flows</td></tr>
</table>

P19-B5 Casa Linda, Inc.

a.

Casa Linda, Inc.

Statement of Cash Flows

For the Year Ended October 31, 19X5

P19-B5   Concluded

P19-B6 Casa Linda, Inc.

a.

Casa Linda, Inc.

Work Sheet for Statement of Cash Flows

For the Year Ended October 31, 19X5

	ACCOUNT BALANCES 10/31/X4	ANALYSIS OF TRANSACTIONS—19X5		ACCOUNT BALANCES 12/31/X5
		DEBIT	CREDIT	
1				
2				
3				
4				
5				
6				
7				
8				
9				
10				
11				
12				
13				
14				
15				
16				
17				
18				
19				
20				
21				
22				
23				
24				
25				
26				
27				
28				
29				
30				
31				
32				
33				
34				
35				
36				
37				

P19-B6 Concluded

b.

	Casa Linda, Inc.
	Statement of Cash Flows
	For the Year Ended October 31, 19X5

EYH19-1   Importance of Cash

EYH19-1   Concluded

EYH19-2 Direct/Indirect Methods

a–c.

EYH19-2 Concluded

EYH19-3 Cash Flows and Bankruptcy

EYH19-3 Concluded

EYH19-4 Nike, Inc./General Mills

a–d.

EYH19-4 Concluded

EYH19-5

a–d.

EYH19-5 Concluded

EYH19-6 Computer World, Inc.

a–e.

EYH19-6 Concluded

CAI19-1 The Coca Cola Company

a–b.

_____

_____

_____

_____

_____

_____

_____

_____

_____

_____

_____

_____

_____

_____

_____

_____

_____

_____

_____

_____

_____

_____

_____

_____

_____

_____

_____

_____

CAI19-1 Concluded

PA-1 Hartman Company

a–f.

PA-1 Concluded

PA-2 Casual Wear

a.

SALES JOURNAL

PAGE

	DATE		CUSTOMER	INVOICE NUMBER	POST REF.	AMOUNT	
1							1
2							2
3							3
4							4
5							5
6							6
7							7
8							8
9							9
10							10
11							11
12							12
13							13
14							14

PURCHASES JOURNAL

PAGE

	DATE		SUPPLIER	INVOICE INFORMATION			POST. REF.	AMOUNT	
				DATE	NO.	TERMS			
1									1
2									2
3									3
4									4
5									5
6									6
7									7
8									8
9									9
10									10
11									11
12									12
13									13

PA-2 Continued

CASH RECEIPTS JOURNAL

PAGE 1

DATE	ACCOUNT	POST REF.	CASH DR.	SALES DISCOUNTS DR.	ACCOUNTS RECEIVABLE CR.	SALES CR.	SUNDRY ACCOUNTS CR. OR (DR.)	
1								1
2								2
3								3
4								4
5								5
6								6
7								7
8								8
9								9
10								10
11								11
12								12
13								13
14								14
15								15
16								16
17								17
18								18
19								19
20								20
21								21
22								22
23								23
24								24
25								25
26								26
27								27
28								28
29								29
30								30
31								31

PA-2 Continued

CASH PAYMENTS JOURNAL

PAGE 1

DATE	CK. NO.	PAYEE	ACCOUNT	POST REF.	CASH CR.	PURCHASE DISCOUNT CR.	ACCTS. PAYABLE DR.	SUNDRY ACCTS. DR. OR (CR.)
1								
2								
3								
4								
5								
6								
7								
8								
9								
10								
11								
12								
13								
14								
15								
16								
17								
18								
19								
20								
21								
22								
23								
24								
25								
26								
27								
28								
29								
30								

PA-2 Continued

JOURNAL

PAGE

	DATE		DESCRIPTION	POST REF.	DEBIT	CREDIT	
1							1
2							2
3							3
4							4
5							5
6							6
7							7
8							8
9							9
10							10
11							11
12							12
13							13
14							14
15							15
16							16
17							17
18							18
19							19
20							20
21							21
22							22
23							23
24							24
25							25
26							26
27							27
28							28
29							29
30							30
31							31
32							32

PA-2 Continued

CASH ACCOUNT 100

DATE	EXPLANATION	POST REF.	DEBIT	CREDIT	BALANCE

ACCOUNTS RECEIVABLE ACCOUNT 110

DATE	EXPLANATION	POST REF.	DEBIT	CREDIT	BALANCE

MERCHANDISE INVENTORY ACCOUNT 120

DATE	EXPLANATION	POST REF.	DEBIT	CREDIT	BALANCE

PA-2 Continued

PREPAID ADVERTISING   ACCOUNT 130

DATE	EXPLANATION	POST REF.	DEBIT	CREDIT	BALANCE

OFFICE EQUIPMENT   ACCOUNT 140

DATE	EXPLANATION	POST REF.	DEBIT	CREDIT	BALANCE

ACCOUNTS PAYABLE   ACCOUNT 200

DATE	EXPLANATION	POST REF.	DEBIT	CREDIT	BALANCE

PA-2 Continued

LOAN PAYABLE

DATE	EXPLANATION	POST REF.	DEBIT	CREDIT	BALANCE

TINA SHARP, CAPITAL

DATE	EXPLANATION	POST REF.	DEBIT	CREDIT	BALANCE

SALES

DATE	EXPLANATION	POST REF.	DEBIT	CREDIT	BALANCE

PA-2 Continued

SALES RETURNS

DATE		EXPLANATION	POST REF.	DEBIT	CREDIT	BALANCE

PURCHASES

DATE		EXPLANATION	POST REF.	DEBIT	CREDIT	BALANCE

PURCHASES RETURNS

DATE		EXPLANATION	POST REF.	DEBIT	CREDIT	BALANCE

PA-2 Continued

PURCHASES DISCOUNTS   ACCOUNT 512

DATE	EXPLANATION	POST REF.	DEBIT	CREDIT	BALANCE

RENT EXPENSE   ACCOUNT 610

DATE	EXPLANATION	POST REF.	DEBIT	CREDIT	BALANCE

SALARIES EXPENSE   ACCOUNT 620

DATE	EXPLANATION	POST REF.	DEBIT	CREDIT	BALANCE

PA-2 Continued

UTILITIES EXPENSE

ACCOUNT 630

DATE		EXPLANATION	POST REF.	DEBIT	CREDIT	BALANCE

INTEREST EXPENSE

ACCOUNT 640

DATE		EXPLANATION	POST REF.	DEBIT	CREDIT	BALANCE

ACCOUNT

DATE		EXPLANATION	POST REF.	DEBIT	CREDIT	BALANCE

PA-2 Continued

ACCOUNTS RECEIVABLE SUBSIDIARY LEDGER

DENVER WOMAN

DATE		EXPLANATION	POST REF.	DEBIT	CREDIT	BALANCE

NAN'S

DATE		EXPLANATION	POST REF.	DEBIT	CREDIT	BALANCE

WILD ONE

DATE		EXPLANATION	POST REF.	DEBIT	CREDIT	BALANCE

PA-2 Continued

ACCOUNTS PAYABLE SUBSIDIARY LEDGER

BRONCO OFFICE SUPPLY

DATE		EXPLANATION	POST REF.	DEBIT	CREDIT	BALANCE

JEANS, INC.

DATE		EXPLANATION	POST REF.	DEBIT	CREDIT	BALANCE

NEW YORK FASHIONS

DATE		EXPLANATION	POST REF.	DEBIT	CREDIT	BALANCE

Name _____

PA-2 Continued

SEASIDE CREATIONS

DATE	EXPLANATION	POST REF.	DEBIT	CREDIT	BALANCE

b.

Casual Wear

Trial Balance

July 31, 19XX

PA-2 Concluded

Casual Wear

Schedule of Accounts Receivable

July 31, 19XX

Casual Wear

Schedule of Accounts Payable

July 31, 19XX

PA-3 Midtown Camera

a–b.

CASH

DATE	EXPLANATION	POST REF.	DEBIT	CREDIT	BALANCE

ACCOUNTS RECEIVABLE

DATE	EXPLANATION	POST REF.	DEBIT	CREDIT	BALANCE

INVENTORY

DATE	EXPLANATION	POST REF.	DEBIT	CREDIT	BALANCE

PA-3 Continued

PREPAID ADVERTISING   ACCOUNT 140

DATE	EXPLANATION	POST REF.	DEBIT	CREDIT	BALANCE

DELIVERY VAN   ACCOUNT 150

DATE	EXPLANATION	POST REF.	DEBIT	CREDIT	BALANCE

ACCOUNTS PAYABLE   ACCOUNT 210

DATE	EXPLANATION	POST REF.	DEBIT	CREDIT	BALANCE

Name _____

PA-3 Continued

LOAN PAYABLE

ACCOUNT 220

DATE	EXPLANATION	POST REF.	DEBIT	CREDIT	BALANCE

DIANE PETTIT, CAPITAL

ACCOUNT 310

DATE	EXPLANATION	POST REF.	DEBIT	CREDIT	BALANCE

DIANE PETTIT, DRAWING

ACCOUNT 320

DATE	EXPLANATION	POST REF.	DEBIT	CREDIT	BALANCE

PA-3 Continued

SALES ACCOUNT 410

DATE		EXPLANATION	POST REF.	DEBIT	CREDIT	BALANCE

SALES DISCOUNTS ACCOUNT 420

DATE		EXPLANATION	POST REF.	DEBIT	CREDIT	BALANCE

SALES RETURNS ACCOUNT 430

DATE		EXPLANATION	POST REF.	DEBIT	CREDIT	BALANCE

PA-3 Continued

MISCELLANEOUS REVENUE

ACCOUNT 450

DATE		EXPLANATION	POST REF.	DEBIT	CREDIT	BALANCE

PURCHASES

ACCOUNT 510

DATE		EXPLANATION	POST REF.	DEBIT	CREDIT	BALANCE

PURCHASES DISCOUNTS

ACCOUNT 520

DATE		EXPLANATION	POST REF.	DEBIT	CREDIT	BALANCE

PA-3 Continued

WAGE EXPENSE

DATE		EXPLANATION	POST REF.	DEBIT	CREDIT	BALANCE

TRAVEL EXPENSE

DATE		EXPLANATION	POST REF.	DEBIT	CREDIT	BALANCE

RENT EXPENSE

DATE		EXPLANATION	POST REF.	DEBIT	CREDIT	BALANCE

PA-3 Continued

UTILITIES EXPENSE   ACCOUNT 560

DATE		EXPLANATION	POST REF.	DEBIT	CREDIT	BALANCE

ACCOUNT

DATE		EXPLANATION	POST REF.	DEBIT	CREDIT	BALANCE

ACCOUNT

DATE		EXPLANATION	POST REF.	DEBIT	CREDIT	BALANCE

PA-3　Continued

ACCOUNTS RECEIVABLE SUBSIDIARY LEDGER

DAVE'S STUDIO

DATE		EXPLANATION	POST REF.	DEBIT	CREDIT	BALANCE

DUKE'S CAMERA SHOP

DATE		EXPLANATION	POST REF.	DEBIT	CREDIT	BALANCE

EVERTSON PHOTO

DATE		EXPLANATION	POST REF.	DEBIT	CREDIT	BALANCE

PA-3 Continued

HAWTHORNE PHOTO SUPPLY

DATE	EXPLANATION	POST REF.	DEBIT	CREDIT	BALANCE

HAY PHOTOGRAPHY

DATE	EXPLANATION	POST REF.	DEBIT	CREDIT	BALANCE

DATE	EXPLANATION	POST REF.	DEBIT	CREDIT	BALANCE

PA-3 Continued

ACCOUNTS PAYABLE SUBSIDIARY LEDGER

POLAROID CORPORATION

DATE		EXPLANATION	POST REF.	DEBIT	CREDIT	BALANCE

TOKYO CAMERA WORKS

DATE		EXPLANATION	POST REF.	DEBIT	CREDIT	BALANCE

DATE		EXPLANATION	POST REF.	DEBIT	CREDIT	BALANCE

PA-3 Continued

b.

SALES JOURNAL   PAGE _____

	DATE		CUSTOMER	INVOICE NUMBER	POST REF.	AMOUNT	
1							1
2							2
3							3
4							4
5							5
6							6
7							7
8							8
9							9
10							10
11							11
12							12
13							13
14							14

PURCHASES JOURNAL   PAGE _____

	DATE		SUPPLIER	INVOICE INFORMATION DATE	NO.	TERMS	POST. REF.	AMOUNT	
1									1
2									2
3									3
4									4
5									5
6									6
7									7
8									8
9									9
10									10
11									11
12									12
13									13

PA-3　Continued

PAGE 27

CASH RECEIPTS JOURNAL

DATE	ACCOUNT	POST REF.	CASH DR.	SALES DISCOUNTS DR.	ACCOUNTS RECEIVABLE CR.	SALES CR.	SUNDRY ACCOUNTS CR. OR (DR.)
1							
2							
3							
4							
5							
6							
7							
8							
9							
10							
11							
12							
13							
14							
15							
16							
17							
18							
19							
20							
21							
22							
23							
24							
25							
26							
27							
28							
29							
30							
31							

PA-3 Continued

PAGE 24

CASH PAYMENTS JOURNAL

DATE	CK. NO.	PAYEE	ACCOUNT	POST REF.	CASH CR.	PURCHASE DISCOUNT CR.	ACCTS. PAYABLE DR.	SUNDRY ACCTS. DR. OR (CR.)
1								
2								
3								
4								
5								
6								
7								
8								
9								
10								
11								
12								
13								
14								
15								
16								
17								
18								
19								
20								
21								
22								
23								
24								
25								
26								
27								
28								
29								
30								

PA-3 Continued

JOURNAL

PAGE _____

	DATE		DESCRIPTION	POST REF.	DEBIT	CREDIT	
1							1
2							2
3							3
4							4
5							5
6							6
7							7
8							8
9							9
10							10
11							11
12							12
13							13
14							14
15							15
16							16
17							17
18							18
19							19
20							20
21							21
22							22
23							23
24							24
25							25
26							26
27							27
28							28
29							29
30							30
31							31
32							32

PA-3 Continued

c.

Midtown Camera Distributors

Trial Balance

December 31, 19XX

PA-3 Concluded

Midtown Camera Distributors

Schedule of Accounts Receivable

December 31, 19XX

Midtown Camera Distributors

Schedule of Accounts Payable

December 31, 19XX